stage makeup

stage makeup

THE ACTOR'S COMPLETE STEP-BY-STEP GUIDE TO TODAY'S TECHNIQUES AND MATERIALS

LAURA THUDIUM

BACK STAGE BOOKS

An imprint of Watson-Guptill Publications/New York

To all my students, past and present.

Acquisitions Editor, Dale Ramsey
Edited by Robbie Capp
Designed by Bob Fillie, Graphiti Graphics
Graphic production by Ellen Greene
Text set in 10-point Dante

Library of Congress Cataloging-in-Publication Data
Thudium, Laura.
         Stage makeup : the actor's complete step-by-step guide
    to today's techniques and materials / Laura Thudium.
              p.   cm.
         Includes bibliographical references and index.
         ISBN 0–8230–8839–1
         1. Theatrical makeup. I. Title.
    PN2068.T48   1999
    792' .027—dc21   98–53214
                                     CIP

Printed in China

First printing, 1999

2 3 4 5 6 7 8 9 / 07 06 05 04 03 02 01 00

ACKNOWLEDGMENTS

I WOULD LIKE TO ACKNOWLEDGE the many people who helped me put this book together and who supported me through this entire process. I have learned that nothing of value is accomplished alone—especially in theater.

First, I greatly appreciate the support my family has shown me not only through this process, but as always: Rosalee Thudium, Richard J. Thudium, Dixie Pasciucco, Richard H. Thudium, Tim Thudium, Deanna Woodside, and their families. Thanks too to all my terrific students at Illinois Wesleyan University who gave their time and energy for this process, and to all my former students and colleagues at Auburn University, where the idea for this book began. And thanks to all my new students and colleagues at Southern Illinois University.

I gratefully acknowledge the support of my production assistant, Shelby Steege, and that of my colleagues Shawn Mallot, Curtis Trout, Sheri Bates, Jean Kerr, Vicki Tinervin, John Ficca, Nancy Loitz, Kelly Ullom, Ken Johnson, Patrick McLane, Darcy Greder, and Kevin Strandberg. My thanks also go to IWU Printing Services, to Chris Kemp, and to John Tobias of the Miller Park Zoo, who provided the lovely animal photos. Many thanks also go to Scott Kemmerer for coming to my aid with his camera for the one group of exercise pictures in the book (the beard series) that I did not personally photograph.

I am also indebted to those who helped me in researching and shaping this book with respect to focus and style: Victor Calligari, head of makeup at the Metropolitan Opera Company; Candace Carrell, professional makeup designer; Vincent Malardi, vice president of Alcone, Inc.; and my good friend Lisa LoCurto. To acknowledge the suppliers who furnished information and product photos, my thanks to Dana Nye, president of Ben Nye, Inc.; Wolfram Langer, president of Kryolan Corp.; and Marty Melnik, owner and president of Mehron, Inc.

And to the Watson-Guptill team who made this book a reality, my grateful thanks go to Dale Ramsey, editor of Back Stage Books and the acquisitions editor for this project; to Robbie Capp, book editor; to Bob Fillie, book designer; and to Ellen Greene, for graphic production.

Finally, thanks are due to all my students who contributed their time and images to making this book possible: Michael Guy Balsley, Brian Bogan, Amy C. Bongard, Laura-Kate Burleson, Linda E. Caisley, Helena Collins, Miranda Crispin, Margaret A. Cummings, James Ensminger, Adam J. Estes, Jordyn Frelk, Anne Gaynor, Kirsten Gronfield, Nicole Hand, Catherine Hoban, Kelly Kirkpatrick, Michelle M. Lombardo, Rebecca Loschen, Kristen McManus, Joy-Denise Moore, Sara Noerper, Christina Norman, Timothy Conan Osborne, Gabrielle Rysula, Sarah Schlinder, Kate Whitton Siepert, Shelby L. Steege, Ben Stephenson, Kate Walker, Kerissa Ward, Jason Weible, Alva Winfrey, Stacey Wooden, and Jamie Zauner.

CONTENTS

PROLOGUE: YOUR ROLE

Before sitting down at your dressing table to create makeup for an acting role, there are a number of questions you should ask yourself about the character you're going to play. Believing that this is an essential first step in creating makeup for any part, I present these "Character Analysis" questions here at the start of the book, and encourage you to refer to the following list whenever you create makeup for any stage role. Ask yourself:

- How old is my character?

- Who is my character's family?

- Where do they live?

- What is their social and economic status?

- How is my character's health?

- What is my character's education?

- What is my character's occupation?

- What are my character's goals and ambitions?

- What are my character's personal traits? Messiness? Talkativeness? Thriftiness? Quick temper? Other?

- What is my character's favorite color, music, clothing, season?

- Who are my character's best friends—and enemies?

Once you've answered these questions and probed the play's script carefully for other clues about your role, you will be in a better position to create the most evocative makeup design for the character you have been cast to play.

INTRODUCTION

MAKEUP IS A TOOL that helps complete the picture begun by costume design. As an actor, you shouldn't appear onstage without at least considering the possibility of what makeup can do to benefit the character you are creating. This is especially true if you're a college-aged actor who needs to be very versatile in your look and who is expected to play a wide range of ages convincingly, and it applies equally to older or more experienced actors. So this book is meant to guide anyone who is truly ready to learn the benefits of stage makeup for the theater.

These pages will take you through the makeup process step by step, from which materials to buy and how to use them, to learning the basic techniques of brush and sponge applications, to designing age makeup and styles of many historic periods. Once the basics of applying highlight and shadow are mastered in our initial exercises, you will be able to create makeup for all sorts of character roles as the book progresses. Simple, direct language and clear color photographs are used throughout in demonstrating makeup techniques and skills. And notice that we've used a flexible binding so that this book may be opened flat on your table for handy reference

while you practice the many makeup exercises it contains.

You will find that I don't make distinctions based on skin color; models of varying colors, races, and ethnic backgrounds are included throughout the book. In my experience, makeup is "colorblind" in that no matter what tone complexion you have, there is a foundation shade to enhance or match it. Highlights, shadows, and other applications are all presented here under the same techniques, without regard to racial or ethnic background.

In preparing this book—after fifteen years of teaching college stage makeup classes—I realized that the missing elements of current popular makeup texts were these: simple instructions, color photographs, and a progressive succession of chapters, each one building on the skills of the one before. I have carefully considered each chapter and its placement chronologically in the book to help you learn and build your makeup skills. Many of my students have contributed to the ideas you find here, an approach that I hope that you will find fresh and inviting. I also hope that costume designers and teachers of stage makeup courses will welcome this textbook as an exciting instructional guide.

getting to know your face

EVEN THOUGH you've seen your face in the mirror thousands of times, have you ever scrutinized its complex structure? Developing detailed knowledge of your unique facial shape and set of features is the first step in the art of designing stage makeup.

Sit facing your makeup mirror with all lights on. Make sure your hair is smoothed off your face and forehead. Analyze by making notes and drawings of what you see.

FACIAL SHAPE, FEATURES, AND QUALITIES

Face Outline Most faces fall into one of six categories or some combination of them: round, oval, heart, square, rectangular, or diamond. Describe yours.

Forehead Shape Foreheads are usually rectangular or triangular, but may be a variation of these geometric shapes. What shape is yours?

Nose Generally triangular or rectangular, also take note of the length, contours, and ball of your nose and the size of your nostrils.

Cheeks Look for prominence, roundness, symmetry, sameness from left to right.

Eyes Determine the width between your eyes, their general shape (almond? round? other?), whether deep-set or heavy-lidded. Are there bags (or lack of) under your eyes? Describe eyebrow shape, arch, color.

Lips Define color, skin quality, width in comparison to your eyes and nose, proximity to your nose and chin, fullness of your upper and lower lips.

Chin Is your chin round or pointed, receding or protruding? Do you have a cleft chin (dimpled)? Note its size in comparison to other features.

Jowls Observe your jawline for squareness or roundness, strength, symmetry, and firmness.

Neck Do you have a long or short neck, narrow or wide? Is the skin taut or loose? Are muscles, tendons, Adam's apple obvious?

Ears Note their size, shape, symmetry, and placement in relation to your eyes and cheeks.

Skin Observe color variations, texture, and how your skin varies from area to area: its tautness, flexibility, oiliness or dryness, pore size.

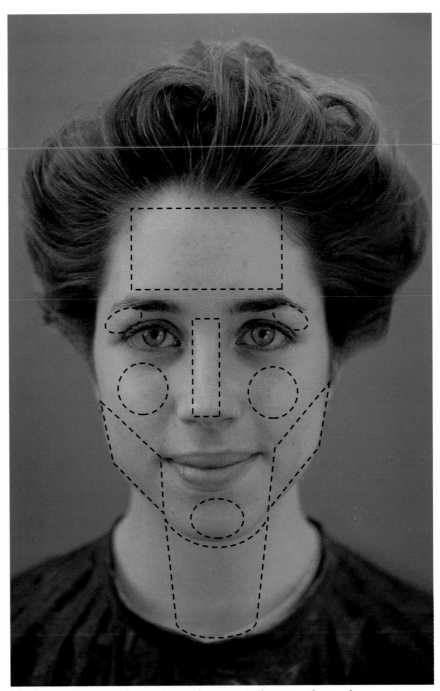

The human face is made up of several geometric shapes, as shown above: rectangular shapes form the forehead, nose, and jaws; ovals between the eyebrows and eyes; circular patterns form cheeks and chin; and a cylindrical shape forms the neck.

EFFECTS OF LIGHT AND SHADOW

When you design makeup for theater, you must always take into account not only the costume design for each actor, but also the lighting designer's concept. Will the production be moody and atmospheric? Will it be bright, cheerful, and happy? Will it reflect the look of real life or will it take on the tones of a tintype in shades of sepia? Any of these choices will affect the colors and styles of makeup you decide upon.

Consider these visual effects of lighting: level of illumination, angle of incidence, direction of light, quality of light. Each one of these effects has an influence on what the audience will know and feel about the play and characters. For example, think of the title character in *Hamlet* at the moment when he first sees his father's ghost. Imagine the lighting scheme for that scene: the level of illumination—low, very dark; angle of incidence—low, to create long shadows cast by objects and actors; direction of light—side and top to allow a three-dimensional effect but to reduce fine features and create harsh shadows; and finally, quality of light—diffused with filters and fog. What choices do you make as a makeup artist/actor to work with this lighting concept? Since facial features will probably not be seen, color may be most important. Silhouette will also be important, so choosing a strong hairstyle may be effective as well. The true art of design—be it scenic, costume, lighting, sound, or makeup—lies in the realm of collaboration. When all team members work together from the beginning, a truly stunning production can emerge.

For a better understanding of the effects lighting has, study the drawing at left. Notice how light plays on geometric, three-dimensional shapes. Practice drawing shapes such as these: a rectangular box, a sphere, a cylinder, and a cone. Set these items on a flat surface three feet from a single light source angled at 45 degrees. Turn off all other lights in the room. Remember to draw what you see, not what you *think* you see. Really observe the depth of shadowing and look for the "hot spot"—the very brightest point of illumination on each shape.

Left: The effects of light and shadow are shown as they play on a rectangular box, sphere, cylinder, and cone. Keep these principles in mind when considering the impact of stage lighting on your makeup design.

MUSCLES AND SKELETAL FORM

The first step in any design requires close observation of your subject, so it's important to study your face carefully in preparing to design stage makeup for it. Certain exercises will show you the flexibility you have in your face and neck and give you a better understanding of the musculature and skeletal structure of your face.

First, sit in front of your makeup mirror and explore your facial skeletal structure:

- Using your fingertips, begin at the top of your forehead, at your hairline, and lightly feel the bony areas of your face: forehead, eye sockets, cheekbones, bridge of your nose, jowls, and chin.

- Close your eyes and repeat above gestures to reinforce the shapes in your mind's eye.

Now, to discover your facial muscles, do these exercises:

- Raise your eyebrows as high as you can, then crunch them down as low as possible.

- Squint your eyes, then open them as wide as possible.

- Scrunch up your nose, then relax it.

- Flare your nostrils, then relax.

- Smile widely, then frown deeply.

- Open your mouth wide, as if you're about to scream.

- Press your lips together tightly, then pucker them as for a kiss.

- Stretch your neck up, then turn your head as far as possible to the left, then the right.

Be sure that you really observe how your muscles react as you do each of the above stretching activities.

your face shape schematic

YOU'LL FIND IT easier and best to design your makeup on paper first, before putting anything on your face. Follow this simple step-by-step process to create your own "Face Shape Schematic," as shown on the following pages. Your schematic—a simplified pattern of your face—can then be photocopied in multiples, giving you a supply to keep on hand for all your future makeup projects.

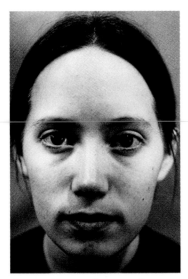

Step 1. Have a photographer or friend who is good with a camera take a tight close-up of your face, using black-and-white film. A 35mm camera is best with a macro or magnifying lens. A black-and-white head shot eliminates concern about skin coloring, tone, and blemishes, allowing you to focus strictly on your features and face shape. Note that an actor's head shot taken professionally doesn't work well for this usage, as such photos are usually retouched to show perfect hair and toothy grins. To create a workable schematic, the object is to get a clear, straight-on photo of yourself wearing no makeup and no smile. Also consider taking a side-view photo as reference for profile designing.

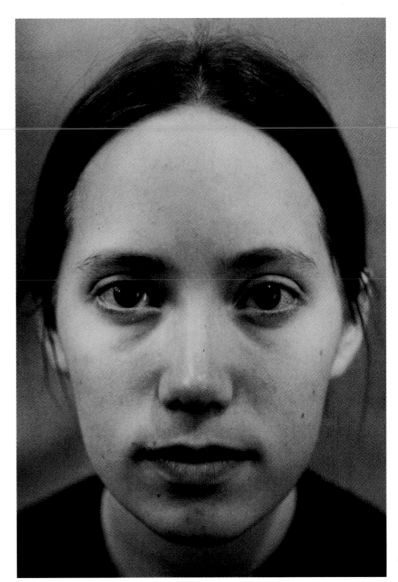

Step 2 . Have a 3 x 5" (or 4 x 6") print made of your photo.

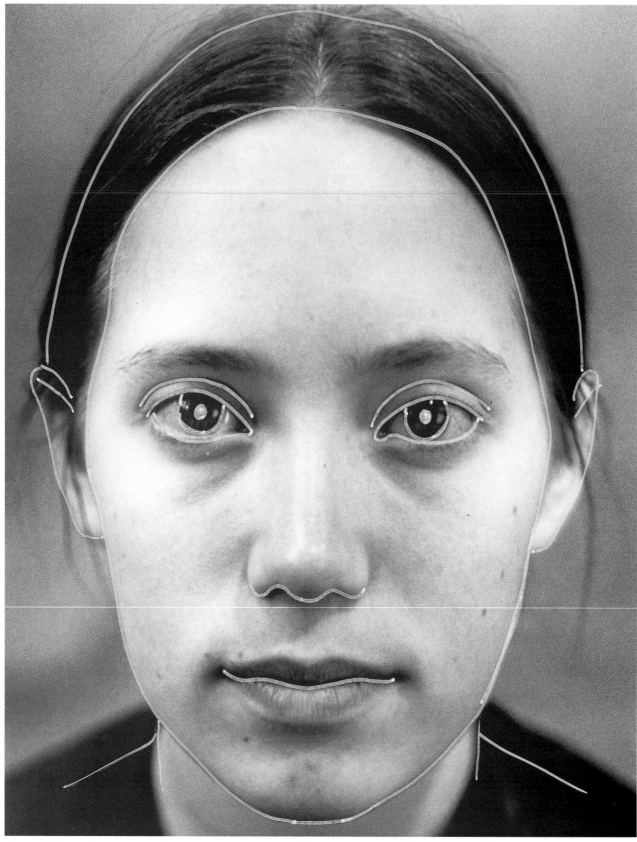

Step 3. Using a photocopier, enlarge your picture 200%. With a 3 x 5" print, you'll get a 6 x 10" blow-up; with a 4 x 6" print, you'll get an 8 x 12" blow-up; either size is serviceable. (Another method is to have the original negative blown up professionally, but that way is more expensive, and I've found photocopies to be just as effective.) Draw around facial features as indicated. Keep it simple: outline of head, forehead line, ears, neck, lip line, bottom of nose, eyes, and lids. The fewer and thinner the lines, the more versatile and useful this design worksheet will be.

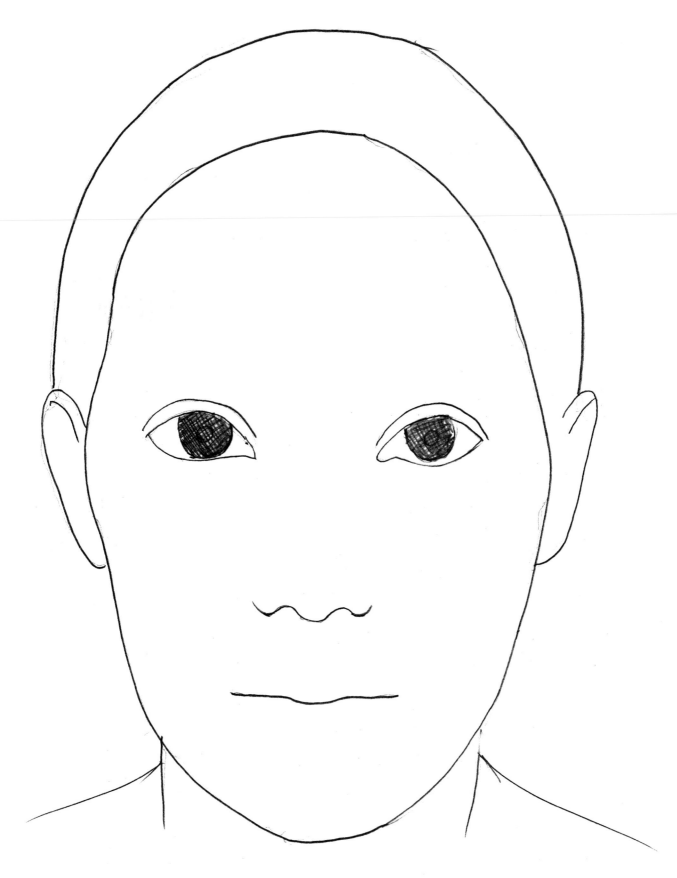

Step 4. Transfer your markings on tracing paper or vellum. Make many photocopies of this line drawing, and your Face Shape Schematic is now ready to be used as the base for all your makeup projects.

CHAPTER 3

supplies and "picture morgue" reference file

SHOWN AND DESCRIBED on these pages are all the items your basic makeup kit should include. If you have trouble finding certain items in your town, contact the suppliers of theatrical makeup (see page 156) for names of retail outlets near you, or inquire about ordering direct from these manufacturers.

At the end of this chapter, we'll discuss the importance of building a collection of photos for ongoing reference in creating a wide range of stage makeup looks.

BEN NYE MAKEUP KIT

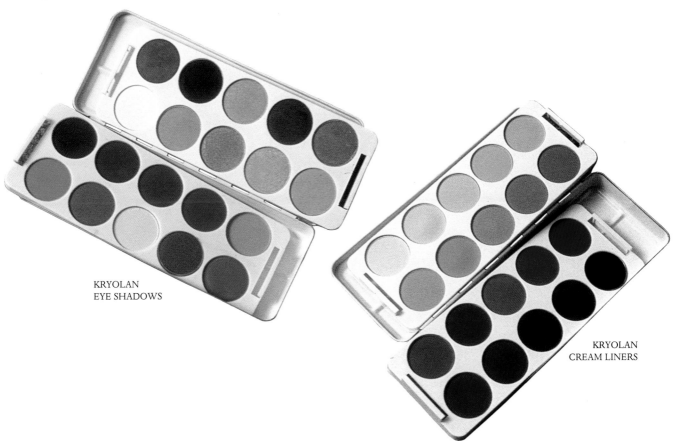

KRYOLAN
EYE SHADOWS

KRYOLAN
CREAM LINERS

BASIC STAGE MAKEUP KIT

The beginning student of stage makeup requires a kit that offers flexibility and is cost effective. No one brand of stage makeup is necessarily superior to another. Each actor/makeup artist will need to experiment with a variety of products to determine the best for his or her skin type, production needs, and personal preferences.

A makeup kit can be purchased fully stocked with all the basics, or you can assemble your own, selecting items from different manufacturers. When you have become competent with makeup products, try experimenting with different name brands and product lines. You may also find commercial cosmetics useful.

In preassembled kits, most name brands are not hypoallergenic, so if you're on medication for severe acne, consult a dermatologist before using any makeup product. For others with sensitive skin, I recommend using Mehron's Celebre kit, which contains a very clean makeup that creates a low incidence of reactivity. It also has an exceptional selection of materials for the price. Another very inclusive student makeup kit is Ben Nye's. I have also used Kryolan's makeup, which has wonderful blendable foundation colors in both cream (Supracolor) and pancake (Aquacolor). Some tools have to be bought separately to accompany this makeup (brushes, spirit gum, sponges, liner pencils).

Now let's review the various items that your kit should contain.

FOUNDATION CREAM CAKES

CREAM LINERS

PENCIL LINERS

LIPLINERS

POWDER BRUSHES

POWDER PUFF AND SPONGES

FOUNDATION

The first makeup that goes on your face (after cleansing) is foundation, which establishes the desired skin tone. A basic kit contains five foundation colors: one color should be your ideal skin tone; the next, two tones lighter; the third, two tones darker; the fourth, a sallow, "old age" color; and the fifth, either a second alternative to your ideal skin tone or clown white. Foundation comes in three general forms: cream, pancake, or greasepaint.

Cream (in cakes or sticks) is the best type for students to use when learning the basics of stage makeup. In my experience, cream applies most easily, and all other products discussed below, such as eyeliners and cream liners, blend well with cream foundation. All the projects in this book have been designed using cream foundation.

Pancake is a dry foundation that requires water and a sponge to apply; it is often chosen for very oily skin because it doesn't promote oiliness; however, other products don't blend easily into pancake foundation. While I don't recommend pancake for beginners, experienced actors like pancake for its matte finish and quick application, and powdering pancake is usually unnecessary (whereas powdering is required with cream or greasepaint).

Greasepaint (in sticks or tubes), although very creamy and movable on the face, is heavy and oily and used less often in today's theater.

HIGHLIGHT CREAM LINERS

Highlight cream liners are used to create a range of

illusions that will be illustrated in the chapters ahead. One off-white highlight cream liner in your kit will serve them all. Clown white foundation may also be used for highlighting, but it's sometimes too stark and can impart a ghostly look to the skin.

SHADOW CREAM LINERS

Shadow cream liners are used for sinking cheeks, shading the sides of the nose, and many other applications. One each red-brown and gray-brown are basic choices. For special effects, blue, red, and yellow liners are useful, as are purple, green, and gray. Metallics in gold and silver are other nice additions to your kit.

ROUGE AND BLUSHER

Cake rouge or blushers sold at cosmetic counters are sometimes as effective as those from theatrical makeup suppliers; however, I prefer the wide variety of colors available from the professionals. Your stage makeup kit should contain at least one professional rouge.

POWDER

Powder is used as the finishing touch to set and keep stage makeup in place. Translucent power is the most versatile for most skin textures and colors. However, powder colors to match skin tones are available, and also consider a neutral white that works equally well for all skin tones and doesn't ruin the bright colors of liners or foundation.

EYE MAKEUP

Both men and women need eye shadow, pencil liners, and mascara for stage work.

CREAM FOUNDATION STICKS

MAKEUP BRUSHES

POWDERS

ROUGES AND BLUSHERS

WAX AND PUTTY

SPIRIT GUM

The eyes are our most expressive feature and should be emphasized for almost any performance role.

In pencil liners, you should have one black and one medium brown for lining your eyes and for use on your eyebrows.

As you progress in your makeup studies, it will be helpful to have eye shadow powders in a variety of colors. For starters, your kit should contain two or three shades, such as a neutral brown or beige, a blue or green, and a gray.

For eyelashes, wand-style mascara is easiest to use. Additionally, women, and sometimes men, may find it necessary to exaggerate eyes further by wearing false eyelashes, which can be purchased at most chain drug stores and other cosmetic counters.

An important reminder: Never share eye makeup products, especially mascara, because of the risk of eye infection.

LIP MAKEUP

When applying stage makeup, lips are outlined and filled in with a pencil liner, often a medium tone in the red family. Maroon pencil lipliner is also a popular choice, but many other shades are available. You might add finishing touches of professional lip rouge or commercial lipstick to give your mouth more color and gloss.

APPLICATORS

Sable makeup brushes used with cream liners are included in most student kits in 1/4" and 1/8" widths. You'll need to add a 1/2" or 3/8" brush for applying makeup to larger areas of your face. Soft, flat brushes sold in art supply stores are fine for this purpose. If the brush handle is too long for makeup application, just cut it down. Discount variety stores carry inexpensive powder brushes, puffs, and sponges. You'll need one brush for powder and one for blusher. Keep extra, clean puffs available at all times. And purchase a bag of triangular, foam makeup sponges for foundation application. Never reuse sponges. Your skin will stay much healthier with a fresh sponge for each project and color used.

SPIRIT GUM AND REMOVER

Spirit gum is a versatile product that will adhere everything, from crepe wool (used for false mustaches and other facial hair) to nose putty. One 1/2-ounce bottle is plenty for the exercises in this book. Water-soluble spirit gum is available, but if you use a product that isn't water-soluble, you'll need spirit gum to remove it; a one-ounce bottle will suffice. A Ben Nye product called Bond Off (for removing collodion, a scar-making liquid) also removes spirit gum. Baby oil, mineral oil, and rubbing alcohol also work well for removal of spirit gum.

LIQUID LATEX

Many student kits include latex, which is used for fabricating wrinkles and other effects. The smallest size available is usually a half ounce, with a brush included. White latex dries clear (when applied in a thin layer) and works better than the flesh-tone variety, which often becomes thick and unusable very quickly. Latex should always be used thin. When it becomes thick or lumpy, discard it.

NOSE PUTTY AND DERMA WAX

Putty is stiffer than wax; however, either will do for enhancing noses and building up other areas of the face. Both come in flesh tones or colorless versions. One small container is all that you'll need.

CLEANSERS AND SKIN-CARE PRODUCTS

All of the following products are easily found at drug stores and other retailers. Thorough cleansing of your face is a must before applying makeup and when removing it, so these items are essentials for your kit.

Cold cream is best for removing makeup. A medium-size jar of any popular brand will do; don't waste money on "designer" cleansers.

Astringent is essential for maintaining clean skin. Witch hazel is an inexpensive choice; however, if you have sensitive skin, you might want to invest in a more expensive product.

Moisturizer is helpful when repeated application of makeup dries the skin, even the oiliest skin; use an oil-free moisturizer daily.

ODDS AND ENDS

Headbands, hairpins, hair spray or gel, comb, brush, T-shirt or work shirt for practice and project days, squares of soft, all-cotton T-shirt fabric for makeup removal, towels, washcloths, facial soap, scissors, lubricating gel—all of these are necessary equipment to round out your kit. Note: Avoid using pre-moistened towels and paper tissues to take off makeup. Being wood-based products, they are somewhat abrasive and might damage delicate skin.

Finally, box all of your supplies in a container that's easy to carry. Try a fishing tackle box, available at local hardware and variety discount stores.

Once your makeup kit is assembled, turn to the Color Mixing Charts (pages 152–155), where you'll find guidelines for experimenting with your foundation and cream liner colors to discover their extent and versatility.

CONSTRUCTING YOUR "PICTURE MORGUE" REFERENCE FILE

Building a makeup "morgue"—a collection of photographs, drawings, paintings, and caricatures—is a never-ending process for the makeup designer, student of makeup, and especially the actor. Having graphic examples at your fingertips of skin textures, face shapes, a wide range of facial types and features, and various hairstyles makes designing for a character quicker and more believable. As you continue to practice makeup techniques, you're sure to find such a collection to be an invaluable resource. Caricatures that emphasize or distort facial features are especially helpful; they can be your most useful examples for character makeup design.

In building your collection, all pictures should be mounted on plain paper, organized by sections as outlined below, and assembled in a three-ring binder. Your pictures should be at least 3 x 5" with the face or feature fully filling that space, where possible. Use a minimum of four full pages per section, unless otherwise noted in the instructions that follow. Color photos are best, although some black-and-white pictures can be useful. Find both male and female subjects. Include these categories in your personal file:

AGE GROUPS
Arranged chronologically, include two pages per age group:

- children: newborn to 12 years
- teenagers: 13 to 19 years
- young adults: 20 to 39 years
- middle-aged: 40 to 59 years
- seniors: 60 years to advanced old age

GENERATIONS
Ideally, use photos of your family—if possible, your gender for four generations to show the aging process. For example: you, your mother, your mother's older sister, your grandmother; or, you as a child, you now, your father, your grandfather. If you cannot use your own family, find four generations of people with similar coloring and facial qualities.

EMOTIONS
Find photos of people expressing different emotions; construct and label one page each for:

- anger
- happiness
- surprise
- fear

FACIAL FEATURES
Examine facial features individually, one page each for:

- eyes
- nose
- mouth
- neck
- skin texture
- hands

HAIR AND FACIAL HAIR
Find the following and devote one page each to:
- three different eyebrow shapes
- three different beard styles
- four different hairstyles (your gender)
- hair loss (four examples of balding)

OCCUPATIONS
The job one performs sometimes affects the character of the face. Find examples for ten of the following twenty occupations:

- cowboy
- priest, minister, or nun
- doctor
- artist
- farmer
- social worker
- astronaut
- athlete
- politician
- construction worker
- biker
- scuba diver
- chef
- soldier or military officer
- car racer
- migrant farm worker
- movie star
- pilot or flight attendant
- lawyer
- waitress or short-order cook

RACIAL/ETHNIC DISTINCTIONS
Find examples of people of the three races: Caucasoid (European ancestry), Negroid (African ancestry), Mongoloid (Asiatic and Oriental ancestry)—then find examples of three distinct ethnic groups within the three races, such as Negroid—African-American, Jamaican, and Ethiopian. Use six pages total.

ANIMALS AND PLANTS
Examples of animals, flowers, insects, and other organic forms will be useful for stylizations and fantasy makeup, both of which are covered in later chapters. Remember to get close-up photos, and include at least four pages.

applying foundation and caring for your skin

BEFORE APPLYING FOUNDATION, to protect your skin, always cleanse well with cold cream, then use astringent, followed by a thin layer of moisturizer as a barrier to stage makeup.

Be sure foundation covers out to your hairline, on your eyes, neck, lips, and ears, using a color that matches your natural skin tone (unless the role calls for a look that differs greatly from your own). For an aged appearance, choose a more sallow tone; for a very youthful look, use foundation with a hint of peach or pink.

APPLY FOUNDATION LIGHTLY

A thin, even cover of base makeup is best. If you lay on a thick layer of foundation, it will result in a blending of foundation color with highlight and shadow colors when they are applied on top. It will also decrease highlight and shadow effectiveness and liveliness of your overall makeup design.

Once your foundation is in place, powder must be applied carefully to set it firmly on your face.

CLEANSING CAVEATS
If your skin breaks out or becomes irritated from using foundation, the culprit is probably not the makeup itself, but failure to cleanse well before applying it and after removing it. Poor diet and sleep habits might also be the source of the problem. If careful cleansing and good eating and sleeping habits are already part of your daily routine but your skin still breaks out, try changing your foundation brand. If your skin problem persists, see a dermatologist.

Another caveat: Never share cosmetics with others. Infections can spread easily from using someone else's makeup, especially eye makeup.

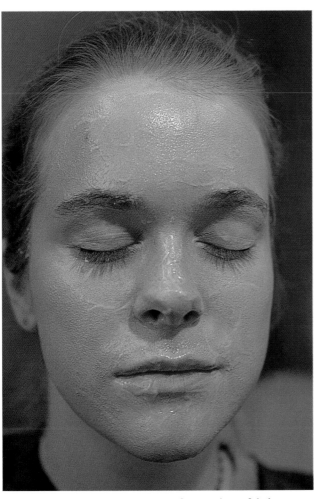

Thorough cleansing always comes first, and careful cleansing is equally important when removing makeup.

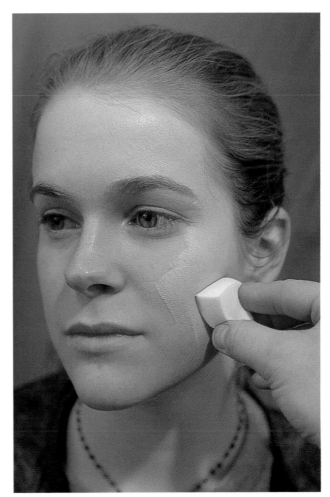

Apply foundation evenly and smoothly with a sponge. Avoid streaks. Properly applied foundation will have a smooth, masklike appearance.

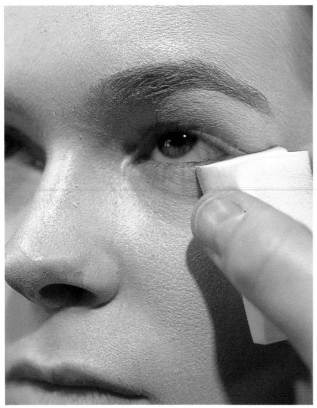

Use the edge of the sponge to get foundation up close to your eyes, right up to the edge of your lower eyelids. Always use a light motion of the hand, especially in the sensitive area near your eyes.

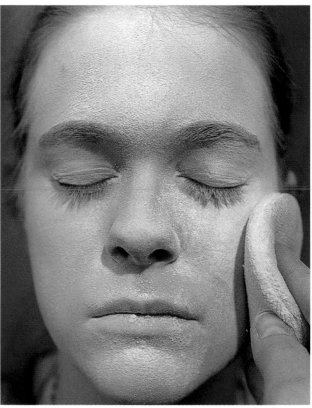

Only after all makeup is applied, pat on plenty of powder with a puff. Don't drag it across the skin; pat gently. A translucent or neutral powder is best for light to medium skin tones; choose darker powders for deeper skin tones.

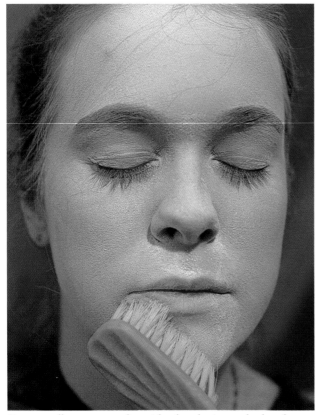

Remove all excess powder with a brush. A powder brush with soft bristles is best to use.

Use a damp sponge to lift any remaining excess powder. This finishing touch serves to set your makeup in place.

MAKEUP REMOVAL AND SKIN CLEANSING

The importance of careful skin care as a regular routine in an actor's life cannot be overstated. How you remove your makeup and cleanse your face will contribute to how well your skin will look and feel on a daily basis, onstage and off.

To remove your makeup, follow this routine faithfully.

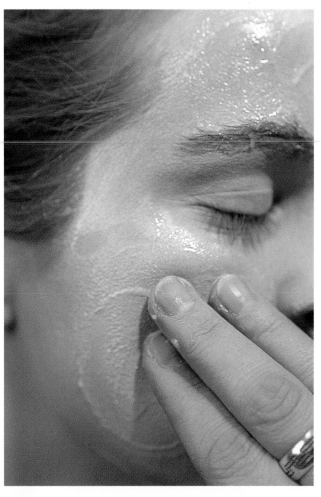

With your fingertips, smooth cold cream over your entire face, using gentle, circular motions until the foundation lifts off your skin into the cream. As cold cream mixes with foundation and the color of the cream is no longer white, a thorough cleansing is taking place.

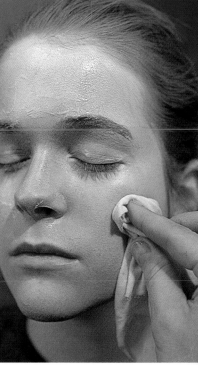

Wipe your face clean with cotton squares. (I usually cut mine from T-shirt fabric). Avoid using tissues or other paper products to clean your skin; many have abrasive properties.

Wash your face with a cleansing soap and washcloth.

Cleanse your pores with an astringent-soaked cotton ball.

Finally, leave your skin refreshed with a thin layer of moisturizer.

CHAPTER 5

highlighting and shadowing

HIGHLIGHT AND SHADOW techniques are the basis for all other makeup applications. When you master these skills, you will be ready to move on to all other projects. As illustrated in the following exercises, these techniques pertain to any and all skin tones and faces.

Although applied separately—highlights first, then shadows—the two effects are complementary, and almost without exception, wherever you apply a highlight, a shadow will be near it. With skillful application, the transition between the two is so subtle, audiences see only a blended, unified look.

CREATING ILLUSIONS WITH HIGHLIGHTS AND SHADOWS

These two genres of make-up—highlight cream liners and shadow cream liners—complement each other on the face. Highlight liners tend to create illusions that emphasize and bring forward certain aspects of the facial plane. Shadow liners are used to recede areas of the face, such as sinking cheeks, or to reduce size, as in narrowing a nose.

Before applying highlights and shadows on your face, practice your design on paper, using your Face Shape Schematic to carry out the following exercise—the procedure you should use for all your makeup.

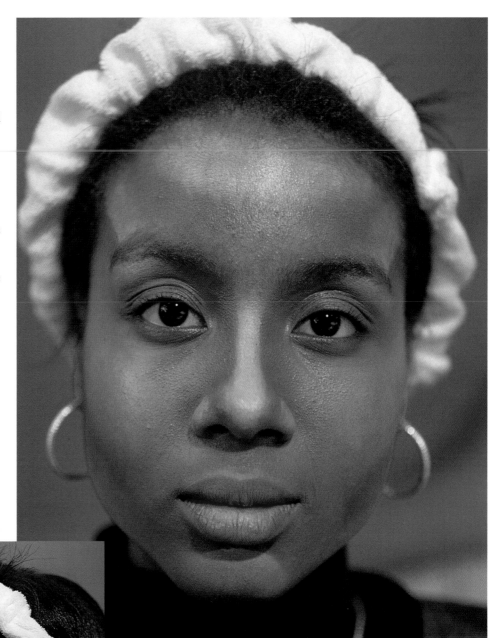

Front and profile views of highlight and shadow applications.

Step 1. Using colored pencils, choose a shade that matches your foundation color as closely as possible. Color in the skin tone on your schematic with this pencil. (Prismacolor pencils and other brands offer a wide range of colors, available at art supply stores.)

Step 2. Create highlights with an eraser and a highlight color. First, erase areas to be highlighted, then tone those areas with a highlight color such as Prismacolor cream or white to make the highlights even more pronounced. Highlight areas are on the forehead, under the brows, on cheeks, nose, chin, and neck.

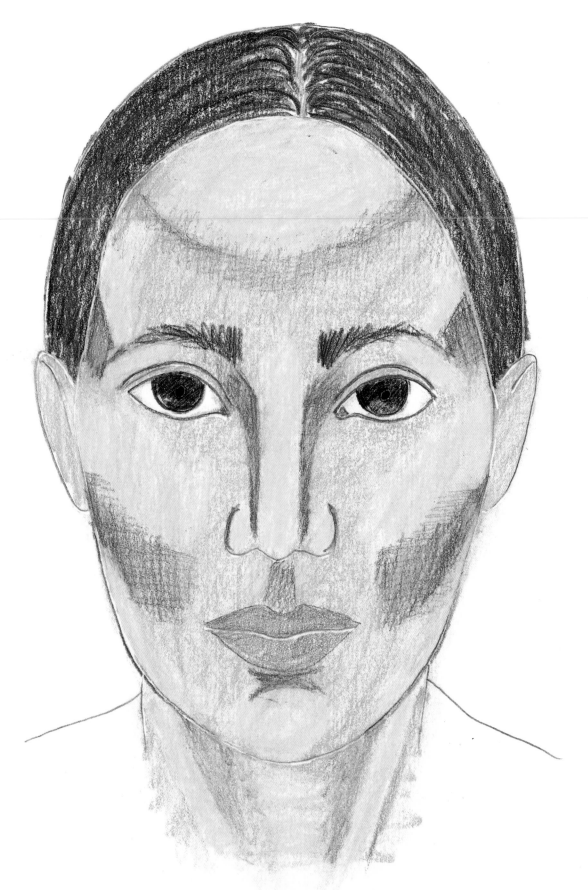

Step 3. Complete your schematic by using brown or gray pencil to suggest shadow areas at the temples, inside corners of the eyes, sides of the nose, hollows of the cheeks, above and below the lips, and on the neck.

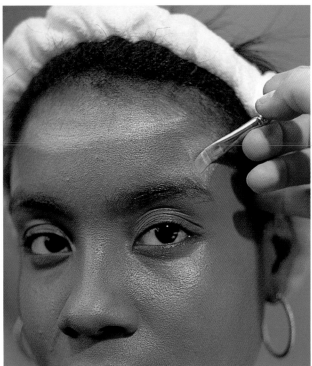

Step 1. After applying foundation evenly to your whole face, as your schematic indicates, begin highlighting from the top: forehead, nose, eyes. Pull up from the line drawn in highlight on your temple bone, using the flat of the brush. Materials used here are off-white highlight cream liner and a 3/8" brush.

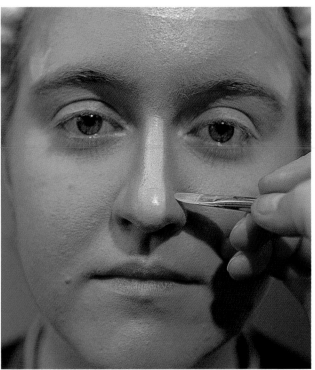

Step 2. Notice how the brush is held differently in applying highlight color in different areas. For this step, the brush edge is held against the nose to create a line on the nostril. In terms of skin tone, as noted earlier, makeup is a "colorblind" art, which I've particularly emphasized here by showing that these techniques pertain to skin tones across the spectrum.

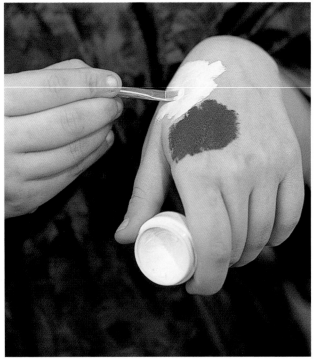

Step 3. Use your hand as a mixing palette for highlight colors. Clean your brush with cold cream after each use. *Never put brushes under water.*

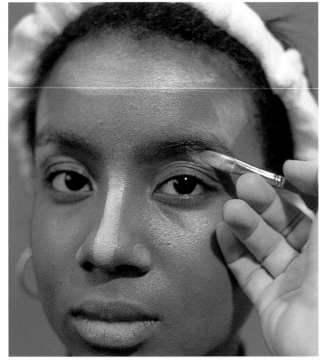

Step 4. Highlight under your eyebrows in an outward direction to given the illusion of opening up the eyes wider. A flat, 3/8" brush is used here.

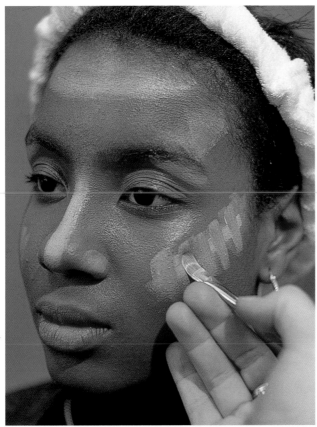

Step 5. Use a crosshatch application on your cheekbones: a long brushstroke, intersected by a series of shorter brushstrokes. Repeat on the other cheek.

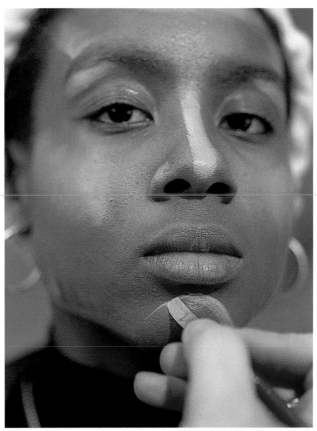

Step 6. Using your brush's bristle edges, draw lines on your chin. Then begin blending your highlighting.

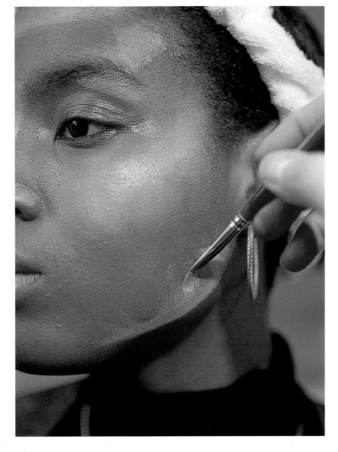

Step 7. Draw a line of highlight along your jawbone, following its natural contours. Pull your highlight up from that line, and blend. Repeat on the other side of your face.

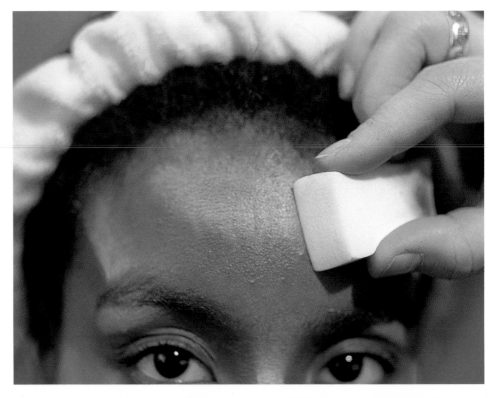

Step 1. Now that all your highlights are in place, start shadowing. Apply shadows beginning at the top of your forehead, and work your way down. Soften shadows with a sponge by patting across the highlight and shadow areas.

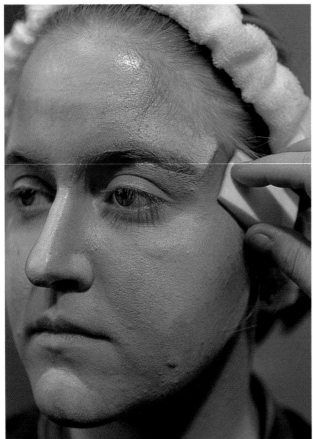

Step 2. Blend the shadow on your temples in a downward direction with a sponge.

Step 3. Apply shadow on the sides of your nose, and blend downward. Use a 1/4" or 3/8" brush.

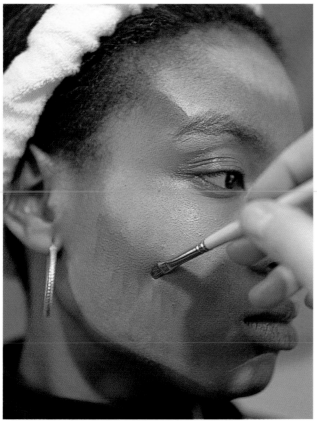

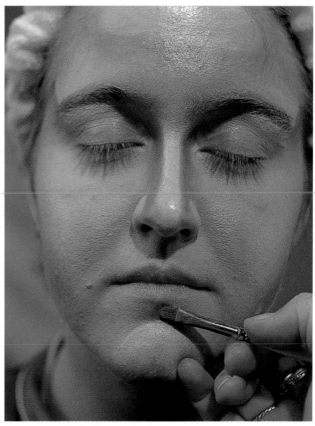

Step 4. Draw a shadow line in the hollow of your cheek below your cheekbone highlight, then crosshatch. Repeat on the other cheek. Continue shadowing mouth area, chin, jowls, and neck.

Step 5. Apply shadow in the indentation below your lower lip, using the flat side of your brush.

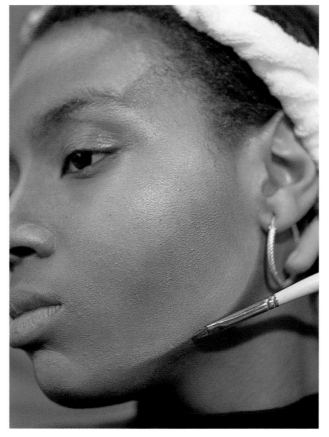

Step 6. Draw a smooth line of shadow below your jaw-line highlight, and pull down from that line. (After each use, clean your brush with cold cream to keep it in good condition. *Never put brushes under water;* it will dry out and separate bristles.)

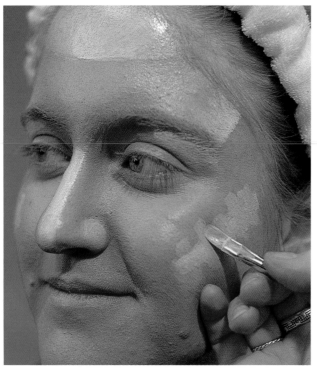

Practice the crosshatch technique by drawing a line and then breaking it up with perpendicular brushstrokes.

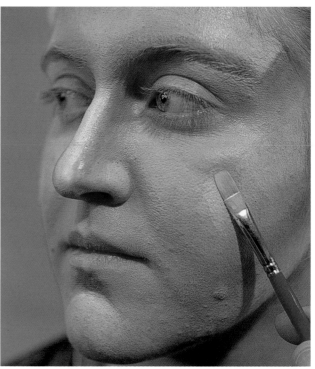

Practice tap blending by lightly tapping the flat of the brush against your skin.

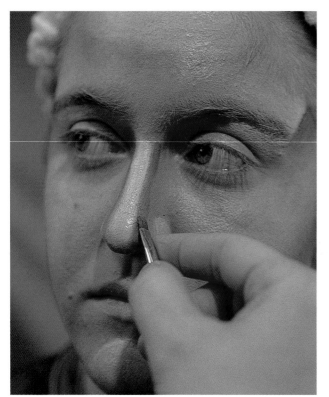

Practice drawing lines by laying the brush flat against your skin, then dragging it along to create a smooth line.

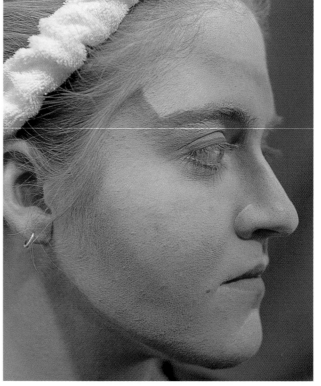

When various brush techniques are fully blended, highlight and shadow areas look smooth and relatively natural.

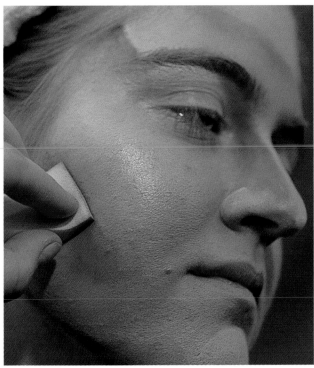

To apply shadow with a sponge, put a small amount of shadow on the sponge, and tap it lightly under your cheekbone.

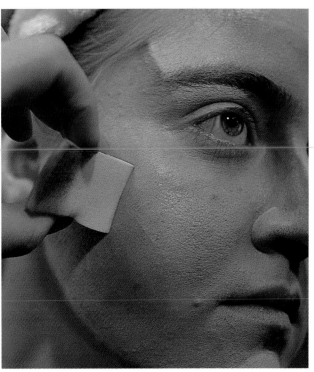

To blend with a sponge, pat it across the break between your highlight and shadow to soften the two colors and create a smooth transition.

To remove color with a sponge, press it against your skin firmly, then lift to remove the unwanted makeup. Correcting little mistakes this way saves you from taking off all your makeup and starting over.

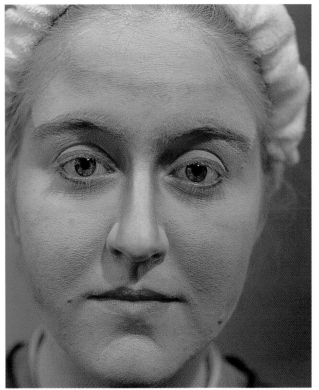

If you put a dab of moisturizer on a clean sponge or a cotton ball, it's even easier to remove small areas of foundation or cream liner. When sponge techniques are fully blended, all colors look fresh and clean. Finish your makeup by powdering.

corrective makeup

WHEN YOU APPLY corrective makeup as an actor, you are not creating a different look for a particular role. Instead, you apply corrective makeup to make your face the best it can be, accentuating the positive and minimizing the negative. While this chapter won't cover every imperfection of facial features that could possibly be corrected, it will address the actor's most common concerns and show how to resolve them, enabling you to put your best face forward whenever you walk onstage.

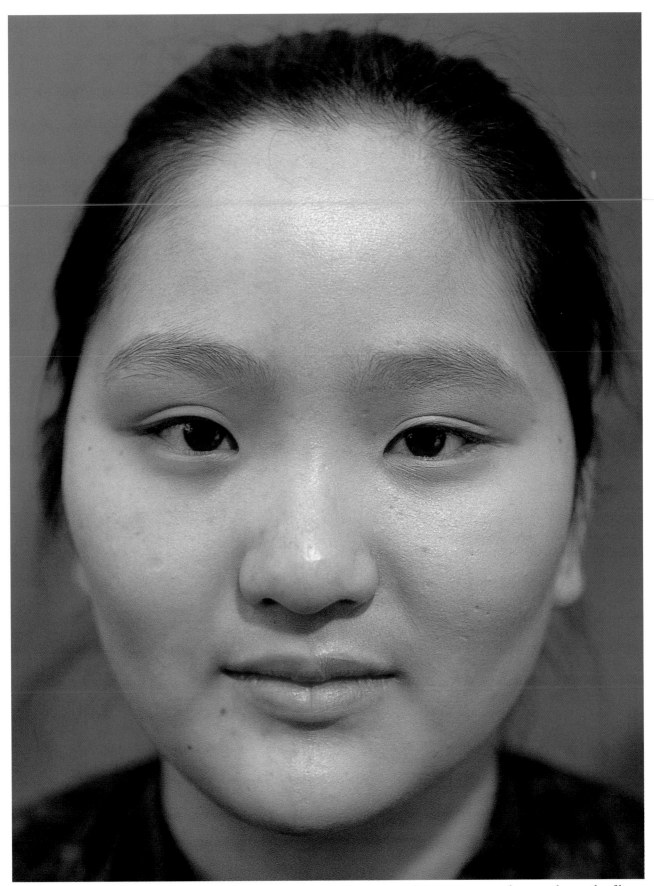

Even beautiful skin like Sara Noerper's may benefit from corrective makeup application. Compare the unmade-up side of her face (above, left) with the subtle corrective application (above, right), where foundation with a yellow undertone (Ben Nye's Japanese) serves to even out variations in Sara's natural skin tone.

PROBLEM AREAS

Using the analysis of your face from Chapter 1 and your Face Shape Schematic, determine which of the six categories that follow include problems that you would like to correct. (Correcting facial stoutness or slimness is covered in the next chapter, not here.) Be mindful of the fact that we all have imperfections in our faces, but not all of them should be altered. Our individuality is what makes us interesting both as actors onstage and in real life.

In the corrective applications that follow, several of my students serve as models. Half of each face is shown without makeup, the other half with the appropriate corrective application in place. As you look at their pictures, the side without makeup is on the viewer's left; with makeup, on the viewer's right.

SKIN COLOR AND TEXTURE

Problems such as uneven skin tone, pimples, "beauty marks," scars, freckles, lines, and wrinkles can generally be covered up with foundation and other camouflage products that cosmetic manufacturers offer for both theatrical and off-stage use. Choosing the right color and applying it carefully is most important.

For Kate Siepert, I blended foundation colors that nearly match her natural complexion (left) and nicely smoothed out her skin texture (right) with a blend of three tones in equal amounts (Ben Nye's Japanese, Mehron's Fair Female, Mehron's Medium Light Olive).

Mike Balsley had some small blemishes and a ruddy complexion (left) that were controlled with a corrective application (right) closely matched to his natural skin tone, a blend of two foundation colors in equal proportion (Mehron's Fair Female and Medium Light Olive).

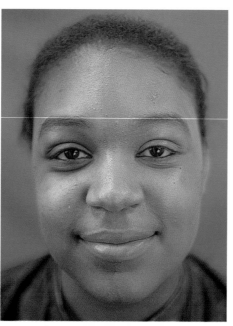

For Joy Moore, to match her natural color (left), I applied a foundation (right) that complements it while smoothing out an uneveness inherent to her skin, using a blend of four different tones (Kryolan's Supracolor 033, NW, 5W, and Camouflage D20).

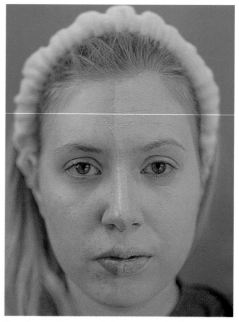

For Anne Gaynor, I chose to make her natural skin tone (left) several shades lighter (right) to create a masklike look, which is quite effective for certain period makeup designs, and also successfully got rid of the dark circles under her eyes and covered small blemishes (Mehron's Soft Peach).

FOREHEAD HEIGHT

If a forehead is very high, by drawing a highlight lower on the forehead and shadowing above, you can create the illusion of a lower forehead.

If a forehead is very low, to create the illusion of raising it (or making a high forehead seem even higher, as in our example), take the highlight into the hairline. Draw the highlight on the temple vertically and bring the shadow up to meet the highlight.

Although not shown in our examples, hairstyle should also be designed to accommodate the illusion of raising or lowering a forehead.

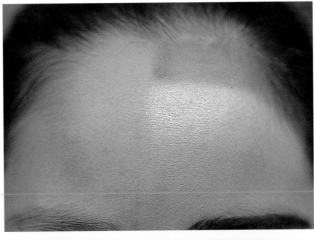

Lower a high forehead with shadowing.

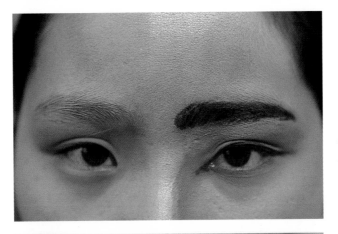

Raise a low forehead or emphasize a high one with highlighting.

WIDE-SET OR CLOSE-SET EYES

To make wide-set eyes seem closer together, apply pencil eyeliner along your lid, extending it inward toward your nose. Also darken and pull your eyebrows in closer to the center of your face.

To make close-set eyes appear farther apart, pull pencil eyeliner toward the outside of your eye, extending it beyond the corner. Reshape and pull your eyebrows farther out to coincide with the extended eyeliner.

Wide-set eyes seem closer together when the liner on eyebrows and lids is drawn close to the nose, beyond the inner corner of the eye.

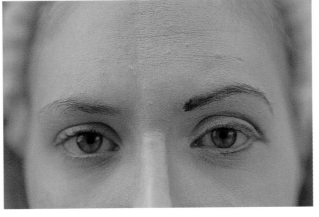

Close-set eyes appear farther apart when lid liner extends beyond the outer corner of the eye, and the eyebrow is raised and extended outward.

NOSE LENGTH AND WIDTH

To lengthen and narrow a short, wide nose: Extend a highlight from the bridge to below the tip of your nose to lengthen; the width of the highlight should be narrower than the actual width of the bridge in order to narrow your nose.

To shorten and widen a long, thin nose: Shadow the curved end of your nose to make it appear shorter; paint a highlight wider than your nose from the bridge down to the top of the curve.

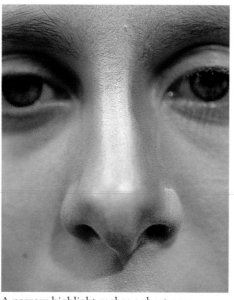 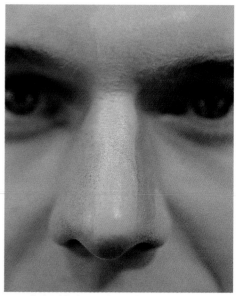

A narrow highlight makes a short nose appear longer.

A wide highlight makes a long nose appear shorter.

PROMINENT OR UNEMPHATIC CHEEKBONES

To lower high, prominent cheekbones, highlight near the bottom of the bone. Shadow directly below the highlight.

To raise low, unemphatic cheekbones, highlight on top of the bone. Shadow immediately below the highlight to emphasize the new prominence.

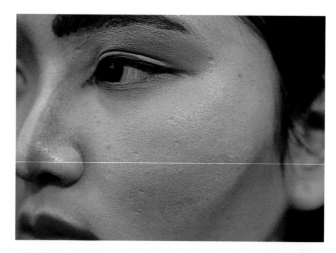

High cheekbones seem lower when highlight is placed on top of the bone.

Low cheekbones seem higher when shadowed below the bone.

ROUNDING OR SQUARING THE JAWLINE

To round a jawline that is too square, draw a highlight on top of your jawbone, curving it in a graceful arc to round the line. Then apply shadow to follow the highlight.

To square a jawline that is very round, draw a corner in highlight directly down from the ear, then apply shadow to follow the highlight.

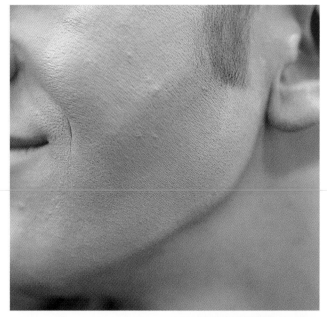

A square jawline seems rounder with highlight applied in an arc on the jawbone.

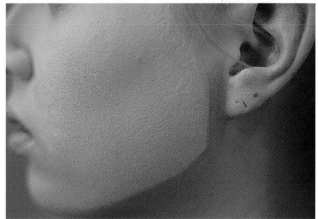

A round jawline seems squarer with shadow applied vertically next to the ear.

ENLARGING OR REDUCING LIP SIZE

To enlarge a small mouth, apply lipliner pencil outside your natural lip line.

To reduce lip size, apply lipliner inside your natural lip line.

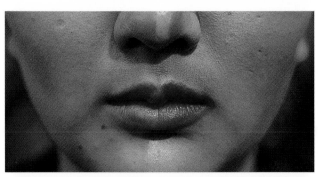

Small lips seem larger when outlined outside the natural lip line.

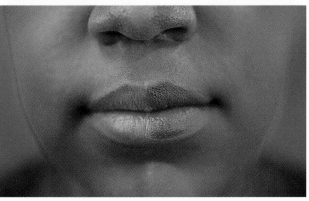

Full lips seem smaller when outlined inside the natural lip line.

STUDYING CORRECTED PROBLEMS

When you practice correcting a problem feature or other area of your face, I suggest that you follow the procedure that I've used here: Correct just half of your face as you work, so that you may observe and compare each application with the uncorrected side of your face as you proceed.

Stand up and move away from your makeup table from time to time, stepping as far back as you can from your mirror to see if the corrective measures you've applied are creating the illusion that you had in mind, and if those effects will be convincing to audiences.

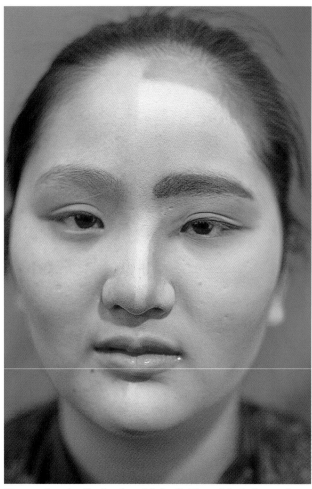 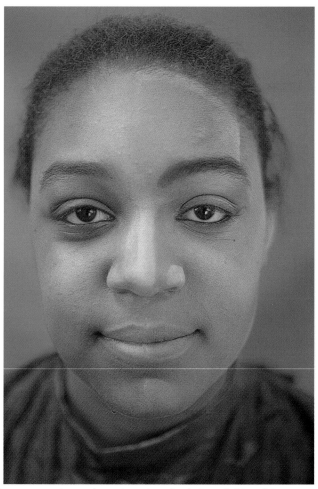

Comparing the "before" and "after" sides of their faces, observe how corrective makeup has given both Sara (left) and Joy (right) a stronger, more compelling look to project to audiences from onstage.

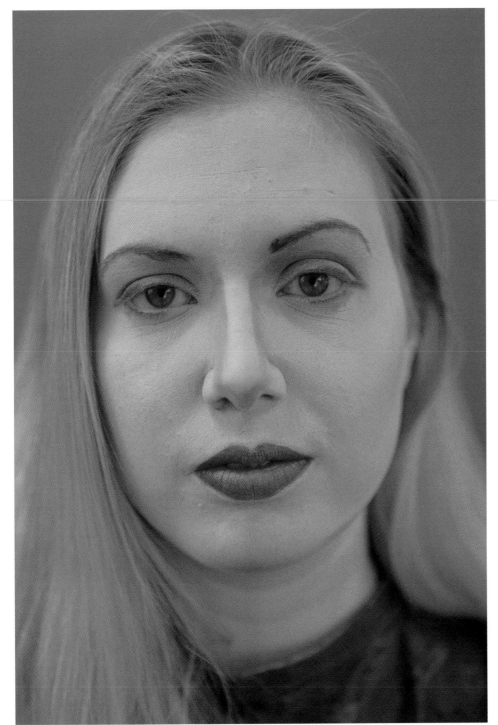

Comparing this photo of Anne in full makeup with her picture shown earlier in this chapter (see page 42, bottom right) shows the positive transformation that a corrective makeup application can produce.

(see page 42, bottom right)

OTHER CORRECTIVE MEASURES

• The costume, if designed properly, can disguise any and all neck problems, and should be considered before a great deal of neck make-up is used.

• Hairstyle can also be used effectively to disguise neck problems. For example: A long neck can be shortened by hair that cuts the neck horizontally; a short neck can be lengthened by either a very short hairstyle that exposes the length of the neck or very long hair that visually reinforces the vertical line.

• If you're an actor with heavy five o'clock shadow, shave closely first, apply astringent to close pores, and apply a foundation lighter than the one you'll use to create your character. Then powder and apply the character foundation.

• If you wear glasses onstage, exaggerate the pencil liner around your eyes a bit to make them more visible to the audience. Since eyebrows, lips, and jowls are going to be more prominent, emphasize them a bit more as well.

CHAPTER 7

OLD-AGE MAKEUP is the most difficult application young actors encounter in the theater. Professionals often enhance stage makeup with prosthetics—artificially created facial features molded of latex and fitted to the face to make a young actor appear much older—especially when advanced old age must be portrayed. However, prosthetics can be both expensive and impractical, and because they are used infrequently outside the professional theater, those techniques are not included. Also, I believe that if you alter you appearance skillfully with pigments alone, your age won't be questioned by your audience. Willing suspension of disbelief is always part of the theatergoer's experience and joy.

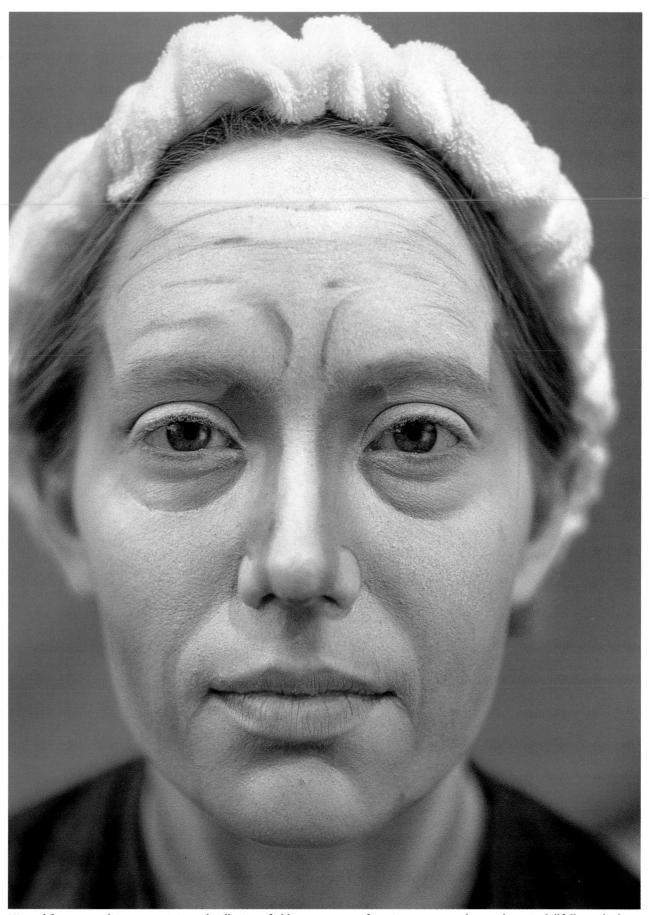

Viewed from an audience perspective, the illusion of old age on young faces is persuasive when makeup is skillfully applied.

AGING PROCESS

How does young skin differ from old skin? First, elasticity of the skin changes. The taut, firm, smooth surface of a twenty-year-old changes slightly by age thirty, but often dramatically by forty-five or fifty, when the skin starts to sag over the jawbone and the neck starts to show signs of slackness under the chin (double chin) and over large muscle groups. Fine lines appear around the eyes, mouth, and on the forehead, and the nasolabial fold—the crease that runs from the nose to the corners of the mouth—becomes more pronounced. Urged ever downward by gravity, the tip of the nose and the earlobes continue to grow (at a relatively slow pace). Along the way, skin color changes gradually from the pink of youth to the sallowness of old age; spots and discoloration may appear due to sun exposure and loss of pigmentation, and skin texture changes from smooth to rough. Finally, eye sockets deepen and darken as the strength of the skeletal form emerges in advanced old age.

Consider these changes and adapt them selectively to your makeup design according to the age of the character you are to play.

FACIAL CHANGES BY DECADE

On the facing page, I've used three photographs of my mother, Rosalee Thudium, to illustrate the varying degrees of physical change a face endures as it moves through time. Comparing these examples and noting the particular changes that occur over many decades will give you a clearer understanding of facial aging and how to portray the process with stage makeup.

In the most general terms, in our twenties, facial skin is usually smooth, almost line-free. By our mid-thirties, fine lines start to appear under the eyes, perhaps near the mouth. In our forties, the nasolabial fold that runs from the nose to the corners of the mouth becomes noticeable. In our fifties, eyelids droop a bit, jawline and neck skin become looser. In our sixties, wrinkles on the forehead, over the upper lip, and deeper nasolabial creases are evident. In our seventies, the nose becomes longer, a double chin appears, and wrinkles become deeper. In our eighties and beyond, eyes sink deeper into their sockets, cheeks sink, and the overall sagging of skin continues.

AGE MAKEUP CUES

• Choose a foundation color that is either more gray or more yellow than your natural complexion.

• Refer to your Color Mixing Chart: Foundation (page 152) and Color Mixing Chart: Cream Liners (page 154) to guide your color choices.

• Before applying foundation all over your face, always test it on a patch of cheek skin to see if your color blend is correct.

• Don't test color blends on your hands; the skin tone of your hands (and other parts of your body) varies greatly from that of your face.

• For highlights in age makeup, I suggest that you use basic highlight cream liner. When you gain more experience, try blending basic highlighter with a purple or gray liner; or try a mixture of clown white foundation with yellow or with green.

• In aging the face, as in all makeup design, highlights and shadows are complementary and are always placed next to each other.

• Age makeup applied expertly on the neck can be the most convincing part of the entire makeup design. But neck skin is very delicate, so don't overdo making it up, especially if the costume is going to cover the neck.

• As with all stage makeup, the last step in age makeup application is powdering the face. It's important to powder your neck as well, to seal in foundation and cream liners and prevent them from staining your stage wardrobe—particularly period costumes that have high necklines or stiff collars that come in contact with neck makeup.

• Age makeup is not gender specific; all steps in the exercises that follow apply to both males and females.

AGE TWENTY-TWO
Facial skin is smooth, almost line-free

AGE FIFTY-SIX
Eyelids droop, looser jawline and neck skin

AGE SEVENTY-ONE
Longer nose, deeper wrinkles, double chin

EXERCISE DESIGNING AGE MAKEUP ON PAPER

Follow these prototypes as you practice using your Face Shape Schematic to begin aging yourself on paper. The application process is the same for women and men.

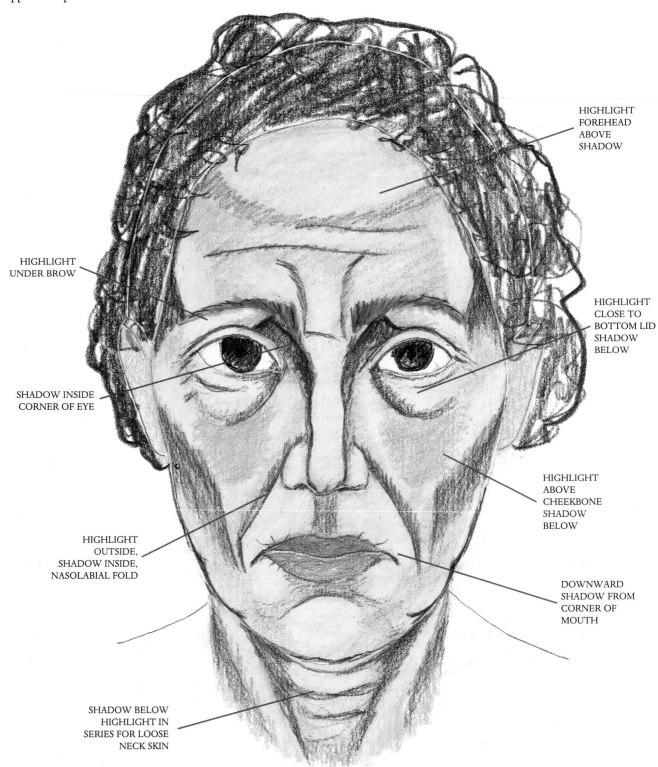

HIGHLIGHT FOREHEAD ABOVE SHADOW

HIGHLIGHT UNDER BROW

HIGHLIGHT CLOSE TO BOTTOM LID SHADOW BELOW

SHADOW INSIDE CORNER OF EYE

HIGHLIGHT ABOVE CHEEKBONE SHADOW BELOW

HIGHLIGHT OUTSIDE, SHADOW INSIDE, NASOLABIAL FOLD

DOWNWARD SHADOW FROM CORNER OF MOUTH

SHADOW BELOW HIGHLIGHT IN SERIES FOR LOOSE NECK SKIN

OLD-AGE SCHEMATIC, FEMALE

Every highlight needs a shadow. Usually the shadow falls below or beside the highlight. Between the two is a blended area of transitional color.

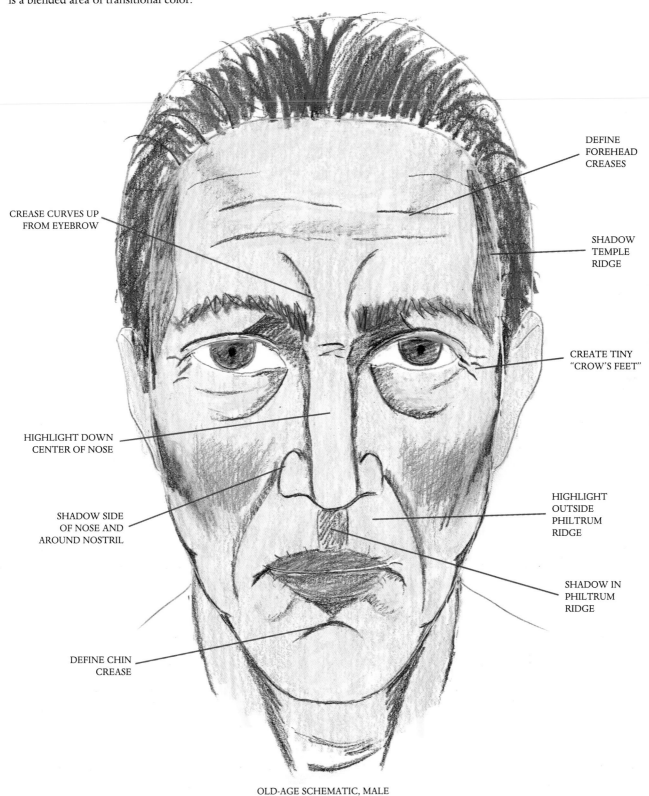

DEFINE FOREHEAD CREASES

SHADOW TEMPLE RIDGE

CREASE CURVES UP FROM EYEBROW

CREATE TINY "CROW'S FEET"

HIGHLIGHT DOWN CENTER OF NOSE

HIGHLIGHT OUTSIDE PHILTRUM RIDGE

SHADOW SIDE OF NOSE AND AROUND NOSTRIL

SHADOW IN PHILTRUM RIDGE

DEFINE CHIN CREASE

OLD-AGE SCHEMATIC, MALE

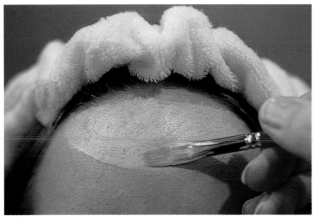

Step 1. After applying a sallow skin tone foundation over your entire face, hold a wide brush flat against your forehead and paint a semi-circle of highlight cream liner near your hairline. This shape will vary with your individual skeletal structure.

Step 2. Add a semi-circular highlight over each eyebrow. To find these areas, frown and then relax. You will see the creases created; highlight outside the creases.

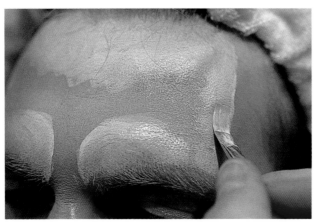

Step 3. Use the flat of your brush to line your temple ridge.

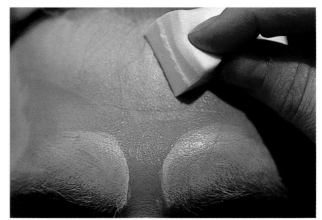

Step 4. Using a sponge, pat to blend the highlight on your forehead.

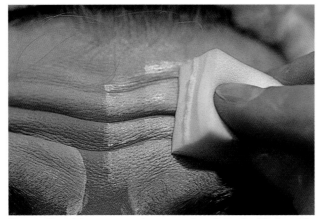

Step 5. By raising your eyebrows and applying highlight with a sponge (or brush), you can simulate natural wrinkles quite convincingly.

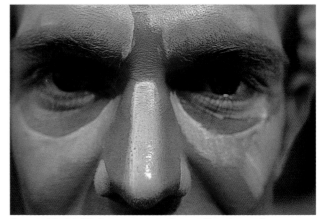

Step 6. To highlight your nose, draw a line down the center and pull it slightly past the tip to lengthen. Paint highlights on your nostrils to broaden your nose, and under your eyes to suggest bags.

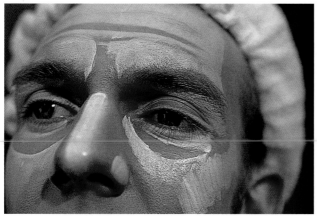

Step 7. Angle a highlight under your eyebrow, and line the edge of your upper lid with highlighter to impart a heavy-lidded effect.

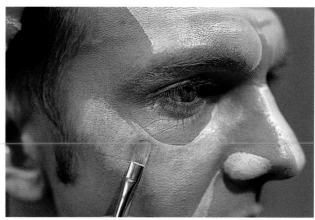

Step 8. Connect your bag highlight to a cheek highlight, then crosshatch out toward your ear.

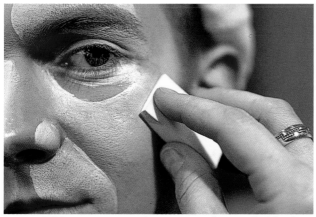

Step 9. With a sponge, use the patting technique for blending across the cheekbone.

Step 10. Blend the hard-edged line laid in to define the nasolabial fold that runs from your nose to the outer corner of your mouth. Find that crease by smiling widely, then relax your face to blend.

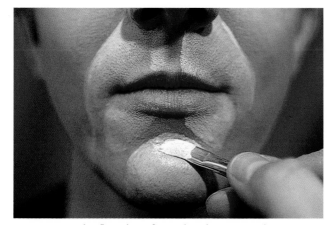

Step 11. Lay the flat edge of your brush on your chin crease to create a highlight. Over your lip, blend by pulling the highlight down, ending at the philtrum (groove above your upper lip).

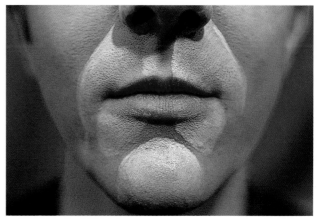

Step 12. All highlights in this area should now be blended before moving along to shadowing.

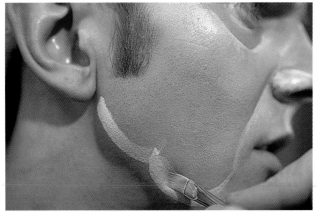

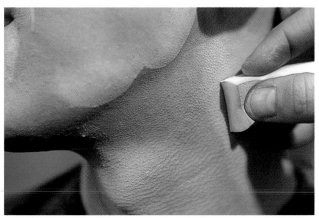

Step 13. Highlight along your jawbone, placing an indentation in the line halfway between your ear and chin. Feel along your jawbone to find this natural indentation.

Step 14. Blend as you go. If you wait until all highlights (and shadows) are applied, the task can be more difficult, and the result uneven. If you haven't blended anything up to this step, stop now and do so.

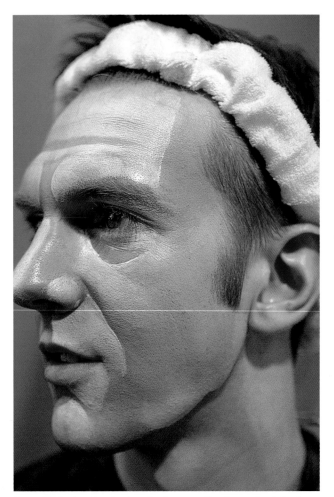

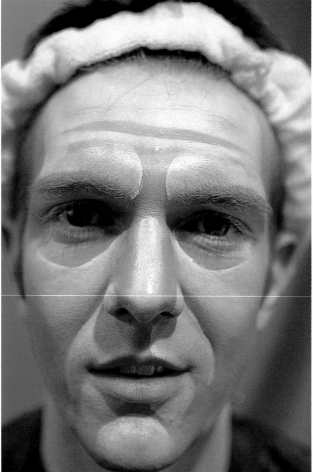

Step 15. Before beginning shadow applications, check both profiles in your makeup mirror to see that all highlights are correctly in place.

Step 16. Your completed pattern of highlight applications should be as distinct as this one, to guide the placement of shadows, which comes next.

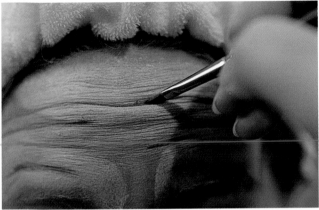

Step 1. Using a small brush and red-brown or gray-brown liner, place fine shadow lines below the highlights that you created to furrow your forehead. .

Step 2. Use the edge of the bristles to lay in frown lines between your eyebrows.

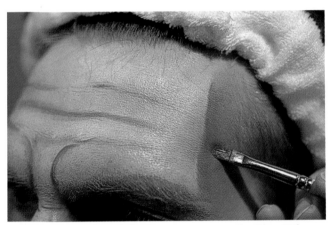

Step 3. Lay in a broad shadow on your temple ridge. When applying shadowing, be careful not to overpower your highlights or allow the two contour colors to mix and become muddy.

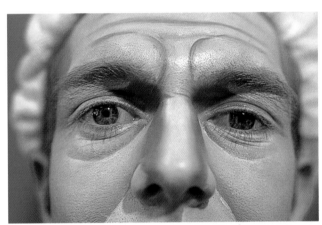

Step 4. To shadow eyes and nose, use small amounts of color, not large patches. Place a fine line in the crease of your eyelid, then shadow the sides of your nose and around your nostrils. Apply shadow to simulate bags under your eyes.

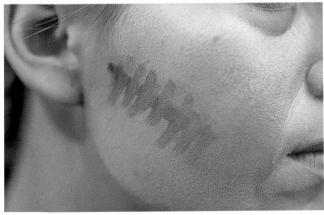

Step 5. To sink in your cheeks, draw a gently curved line in the hollow of your cheek and crosshatch through it.

Step 6. Shade the cheek, using a sponge to tone and blend.

CHAPTER 8

facial stoutness and slimness

NOW THAT YOU UNDERSTAND the techniques of highlighting and shadowing to create age makeup, you will be able to apply those principles to the projects in this and the following chapters. Let's begin by putting your newfound techniques to work to develop an illusion of facial stoutness or slimness.

If you are cast to play a character whose weight differs somewhat from yours, the costume designer may help increase or reduce your size by building a "fat" suit or by corseting you in some fashion. Then, as the actor or makeup designer, it's your job to take that illusion further by creating the appropriate look of weight in the face.

EXAGGERATING OR MINIMIZING FACIAL TRAITS

There are several facial areas to consider in terms of weight. Any part of your face can be adjusted with the use of make-up to contribute to an impression of stoutness or slimness: the height and width of your forehead; the smallness or largness of your eyes and their spacing and fleshiness; whether your cheekbones are prominent or unnoticeable; whether your lips are full or thin; and how long or short your neck appears to be.

Once you have considered each of these areas carefully, you may begin exaggerating or minimizing features to correspond to either the stout or slim look called for by your role.

Follow the steps below to create a thin side and a stout side of your face, as demonstrated. It's good to practice both at the same time to compare and contrast the differences. I've chosen two models, one female and relatively slim, the other, male, and relatively stout. For each we create a stout side (on the viewer's left) and a thin side (on the viewer's right).

Study this schematic for stoutness (left) and slimness (right) as preparation for the exercise that follows, where you will create a slim side and a stout side of your face.

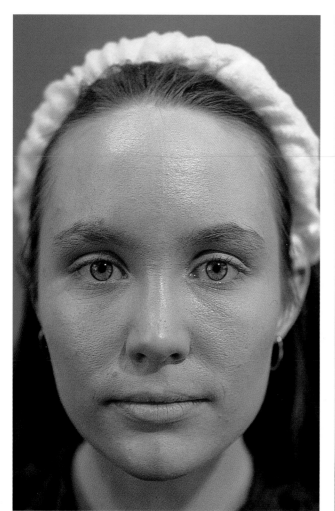 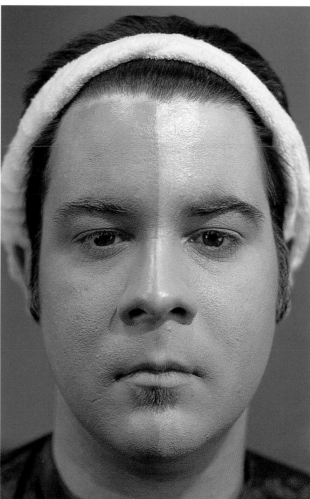

Step 1. Foundation: Divide your face down the center with foundation. The stout side (left on both faces) should be warmer. The thin side (right on both faces), more sallow in tone.

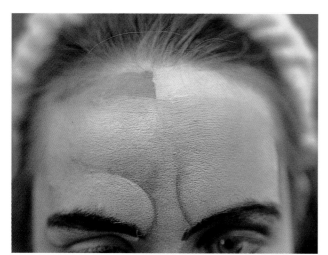 

Step 2. Forehead: The stout forehead is lowered, widened, and made fuller over the eyes. The forehead on the slim side is raised, narrowed, and made less full over the eyes.

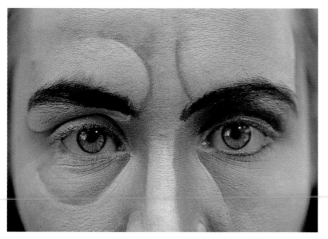
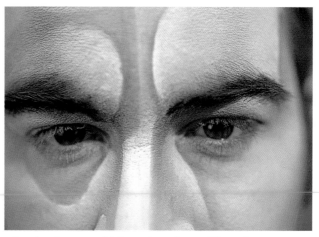

Step 3. Eyes: The eye on the stout side is full over and under the eye, with large bags, heavy lids, and short, heavy eyebrows added. On the slim side, the eye is highlighted only toward the outside; the bag is vertical, and there are heavy shadows under the arched, thin eyebrow.

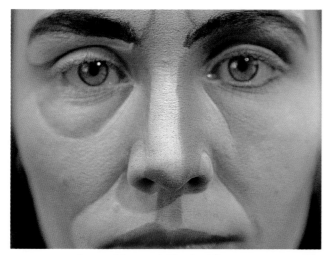

Step 4. Nose and Cheeks: The stout nose is widened and given large nostrils; the stout cheeks are heavily highlighted—no shadowing. The slim nose is lengthened, narrowed, and give angled, sharp nostrils; the slim cheeks are sunken and shadowed with high cheekbones.

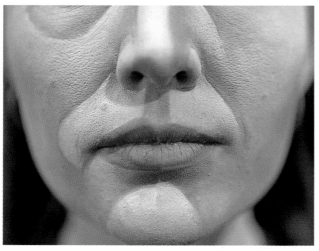
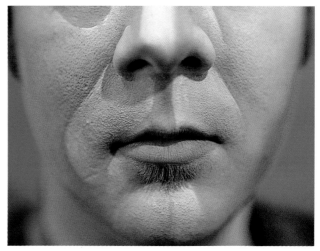

Step 5. Nasolabial Folds, Lips, and Chin: On the stout side the mouth has a curved, full nasolabial line, oversized lips, and a curved crease line above the upper lip; the chin is low and wide. On the slim side, the mouth has a shorter, more vertical nasolabial fold; the lips are drawn inside the lip line, and the crease line above the lip is long and straight; the chin is high and arched.

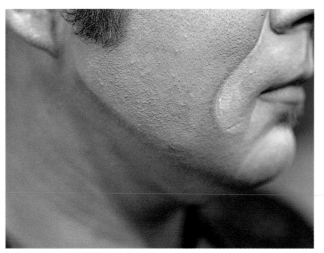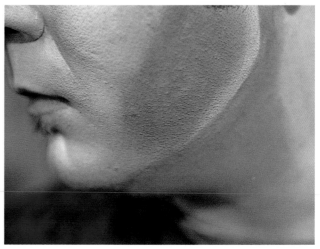

Step 6. Jawline (photos, male only): Left, on the stout side the jawline is rounded and full. Right, on the slim side the jawline is square and sharp.

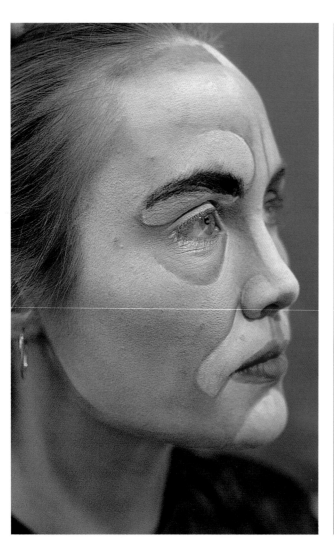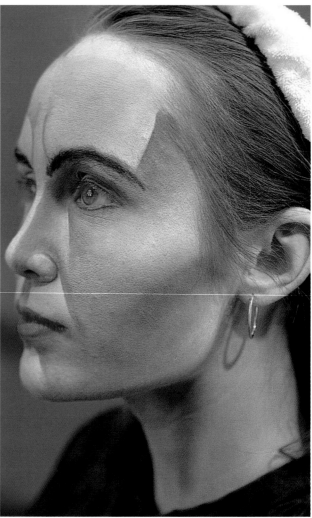

Step 7. The stout side (left) and slim side (right) of our female model are now completed.

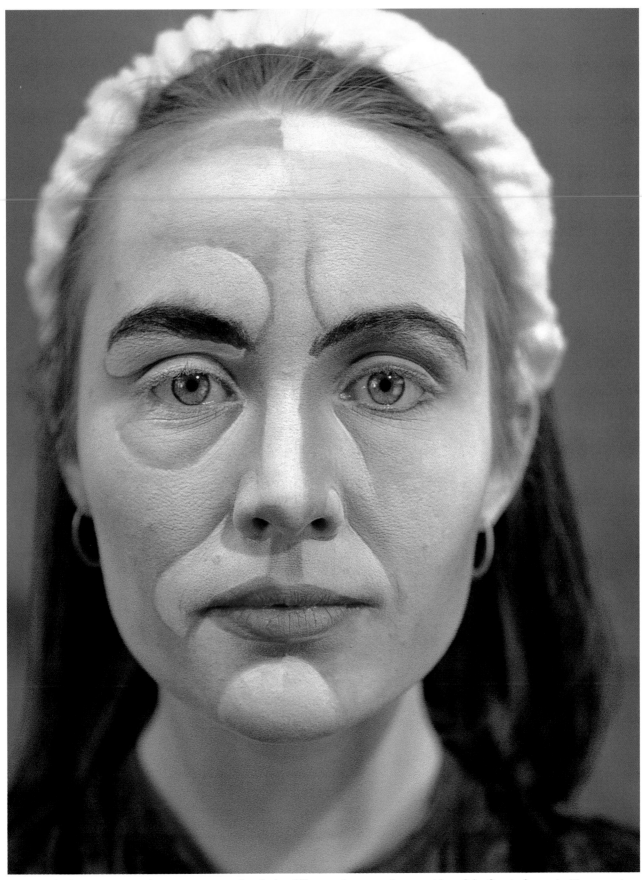

Step 8. The last step is powdering. Now completed, the difference between the two sides of the face is dramatic. To appreciate the full effect, cover the right half of this photo with a sheet of paper and study the stout side, then cover the left side of the photo to study the slim side.

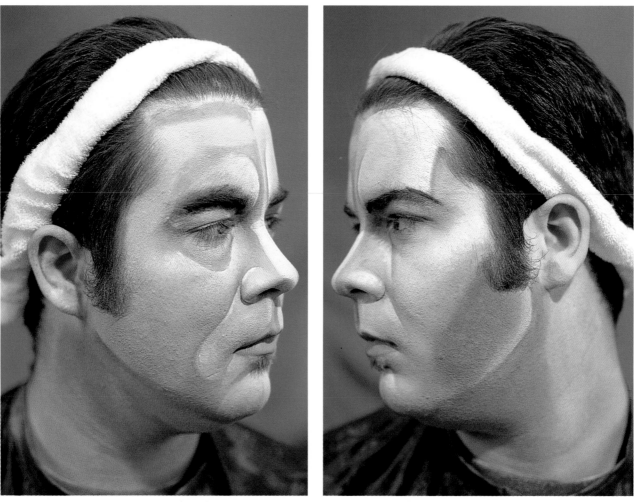

Step 9. The stout side (left) and slim side (right) of our male model are now completed.

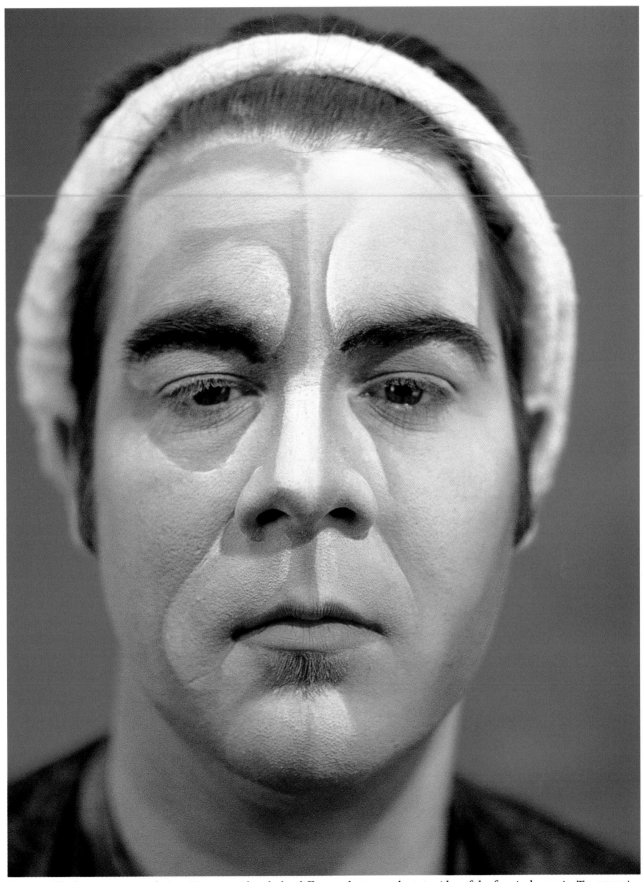

Step 10. The last step is powdering. Now completed, the difference between the two sides of the face is dramatic. To appreciate the full effect, cover the right half of this photo with a sheet of paper and study the stout side, then cover the left side of the photo to study the slim side.

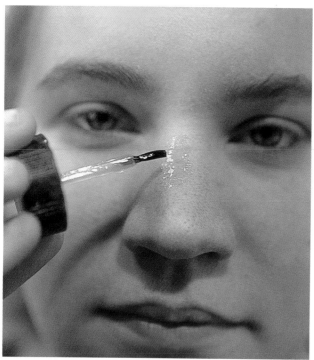

Step 1. Apply spirit gum to the area of your bumpy bruise. Spirit gum will securely adhere nose putty or derma wax to your skin. (This exercise uses derma wax.)

Step 2. Scoop out the desired amount of derma wax and roll it in your hands until it's soft and ball-shaped. If the wax sticks to your fingers, rub lubricating gel on your hands to keep your fingers slick and the wax soft and not sticky.

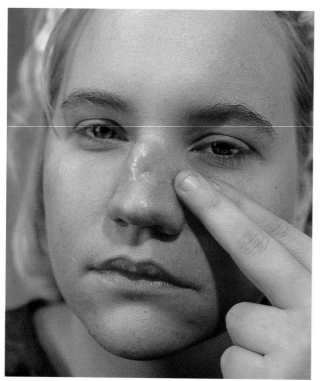

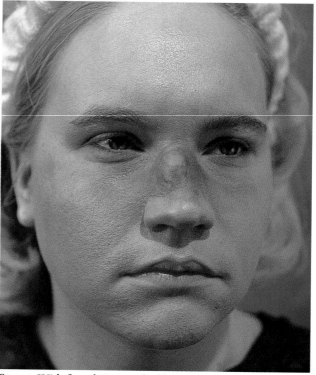

Step 3. Once the wax is secured to the bony spot, with lubricating gel on your fingertips, smooth out the ball into whatever shape wound you wish to create.

Step 4. With foundation applied by sponge over the wax and on your entire face, begin painting the wound with maroon and purple cream liners to simulate a fresh bruise. (For an older bruise already healing, use green and yellow liners.)

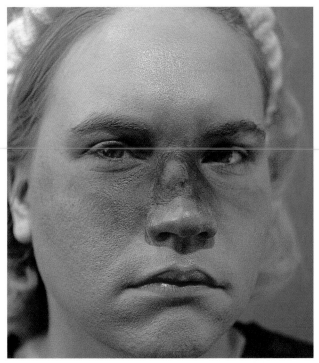

Step 5. Since discoloration usually spreads beyond the site of a blow, continue patting on purple and maroon liners with a sponge, extending the color beyond the bumpy bruise on your nose.

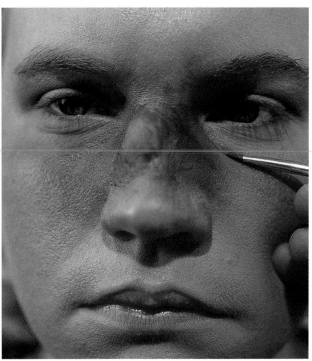

Step 6. When your nose is severly damaged, both eyes will suffer. Using a brush now with your maroon liner, paint in bruised veins under both eyes, in the bag area.

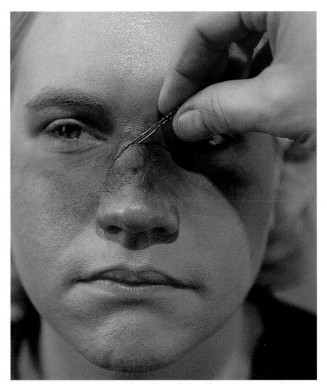

Step 7. Once the bruised and swollen effect is acheived, using the blunt end of a hairpin, cut through the putty to produce a split-skin effect. Angle the cut so it's wide enough to have stage blood inserted into it.

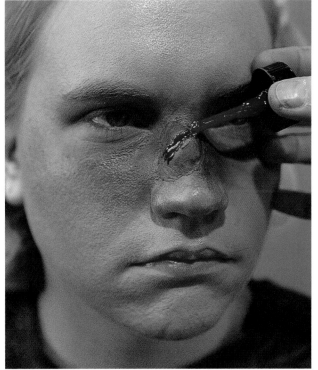

Step 8. After lightly dusting the wound area with powder to set the makeup and dry the wax so that blood will stick to it, apply "thick" stage blood into the slit you opened in the previous step.

NEW SCAR: Step 1. To create a more recent scar, raised higher above the skin, paint clear liquid latex on a piece of glass or any smooth, nonporous surface, shaping the latex into the type of scar you want. Let the latex dry thoroughly to the point of being faintly yellow in color. ("Clear" latex dries clear only when applied on skin in a very thin layer.)

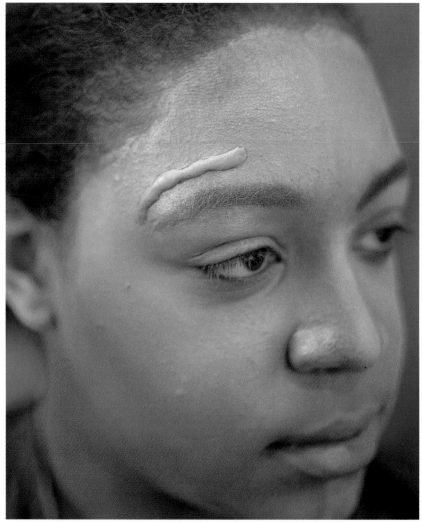

Step 2. Apply spirit gum on the spot where the scar is to be affixed. Allow both the spirit gum and your latex piece to feel tacky to the touch before attaching the scar.

Step 3. Finish with highlights and shadows. A touch of maroon cream liner on the scar aids believability.

OLD SCAR: The first step is brushing on collodion, a viscous solution that shrinks as it dries. The ridge shown, applied to the model's freshly cleansed face, is the result. Once the next step is completed—applying foundation, highlight, shadow, and powder over it—from an audience perspective, it will look just like an old scar.

Step 1. Using a sponge, apply a thin layer of liquid latex to the desired area. Allow the latex to dry thoroughly. If you want the look of thicker skin in the burn area, add more latex. (For latex application, see Chapter 7.)

Step 2. Allow the latex to dry thoroughly. Notice the deep wrinkles achieved with several layers of latex applied.

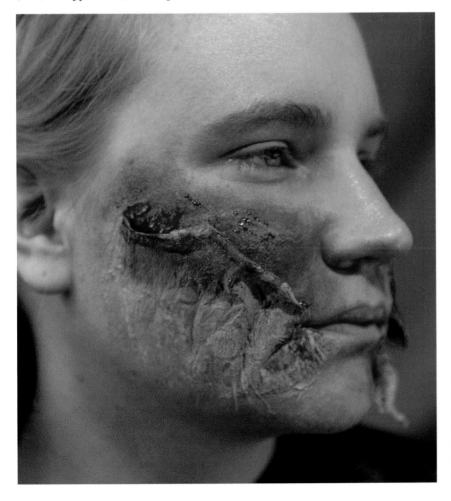

Step 3. Roll back parts of the latex to simulate the peeling, roughed-up look of burned skin. Paint with foundation and cream liners. Stipple maroon, blue, and black cream liner around the burn. For an even more realistic and gory look, add stage blood.

CHAPTER 10

period makeup

ACTORS ARE OFTEN expected to play period roles, ranging from the Greek classics through Shakespeare, Molière, and Ibsen to works by early greats of our own century, such as Shaw and Coward. When preparing to play a period role, students shouldn't rely solely on the costume designer to establish a character's appearance. If you do your own research about the period, guided by the following pages, you'll be much better equipped to contribute to the design of your character's makeup and hairstyle.

Strong, symmetrical facial features are called for in designing makeup for a classical Greek role.

BUILDING YOUR REPERTORY OF MAKEUP STYLES

Assembled here are makeup guidelines for some of the most frequently chosen time periods of plays performed in American theater, beginning with classical Greek and ending in the twentieth century. Rather than delineating every conceivable time frame, I've chosen those periods for which I have especially enjoyed designing costumes and makeup. Only two eras in our own century are included, because design research for other decades is quite accessible and straightforward enough for you to develop your own prototypes.

In practicing period makeup, choose an era that appeals to you, and then follow these steps:

• Find a play set in the period you've chosen. (For each era in my examples, play titles are suggested.)

•. Read the play and select the character you'd like to portray

• Write a brief character analysis for your role (see page 8 for guidelines).

• Research the fashion and makeup styles, mores, social and economic conditions, and the play's geographic setting.

• Based on the information you've now gathered, design your makeup on paper, then create the design on your face.

GREEK SCHEMATIC, MALE

CLASSICAL GREEK

The Greeks loved symmetry and proportion in a human face. Those principles are best expressed with a makeup design that lines up the corners of your mouth with the pupils of your eyes and creates a space between your eyes equal to the width of one eye. Make your nose length equal to two eye widths, and be sure that all your features are youthful and strong. These characteristics are essentially the same for male or female.

Recommended plays: By Sophocles, *Oedipus, Antigone;* by Euripides, *Trojan Women, Medea;* by Aristophanes, *The Birds, Lysistrata.*

GREEK SCHEMATIC, FEMALE

GREEK MAKEUP, FEMALE

RENAISSANCE

The fifteenth and sixteenth centuries were years of greatness on many levels, notably the discovery and exploration of the Americas and the flourishing of art by Botticelli, Leonardo da Vinci, Raphael, Michaelangelo, Titian, and other masters. Fashions of the day reflected this period of rebirth and new thinking. Men's clothing was typically broad in structure with horizontal emphasis. Faces, too, were broad and strong; many portraits of Italian men show hooded eyes, dark eyebrows, and long, aquiline noses on clean-shaven faces, the style I've chosen for the model you see here. Women's portraits, exemplified by portrayals of the Madonna, were often painted with angelic expressions, pale skin, soft eyes, small lips, and long necks.

Recommended plays: By William Shakespeare, *Two Gentlemen of Verona, The Merchant of Venice, Romeo and Juliet, The Taming of the Shrew;* by Carlo Goldoni, *The Venetian Twins;* by Niccoló Machiavelli, *La Mandragola.*

RENAISSANCE SCHEMATIC, MALE

RENAISSANCE MAKEUP, MALE

RENAISSANCE SCHEMATIC, FEMALE

RENAISSANCE MAKEUP, FEMALE

ELIZABETHAN

Queen Elizabeth I truly set the style for how the nobility in England and many other countries dressed during the sixteenth century. Men wore heavy, jewel-encrusted garments, ruffs, breeches, light stockings, and plenty of rings. Women also wore heavy fabrics and ruffs, farthengales to expand and stiffen their skirts, and lots of pearls. Such fashions may be seen in paintings by Nicholas Hilliard, Hans Holbein the Younger, and other artists of the period. Makeup, not widely used since ancient cultures, became part of Elizabeth's daily routine. Her primary foundation was white lead, which actually increased the speed of a woman's fading beauty because of its side effect of eating away at the skin's surface and in many cases hastening the death of the wearer. Unfortunately, courtiers and many women of fashion around the world chose to follow the queen's example, with dire results.

Recommended plays: By Shakespeare, *Twelfth Night, Hamlet, The Merry Wives of Windsor, As You Like It*; by Ben Jonson, *Every Man in His Humour*; by Christopher Marlowe, *Dr. Faustus*.

ELIZABETHAN SCHEMATIC, MALE

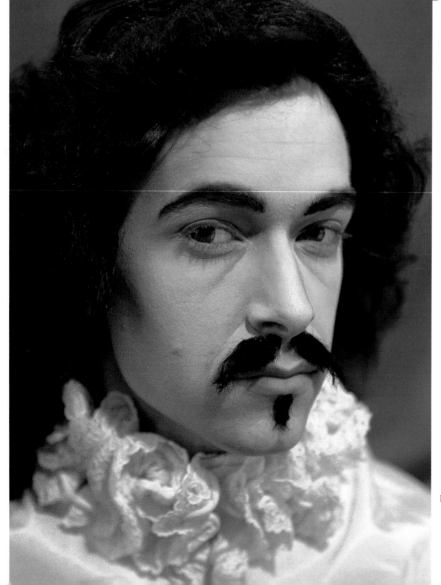

ELIZABETHAN MAKEUP, MALE

ELIZABETHAN SCHEMATIC, FEMALE

ELIZABETHAN MAKEUP, FEMALE

PERIOD MAKEUP 87

RESTORATION AND EIGHTEENTH CENTURY

What a glorious period for makeup! Featured were white rice powder, rouge for men's and women's cheeks and lips, and wigs that took on a life of their own. Beauty marks in the form of little black leather patches shaped like moons, stars, and hearts were placed on the most aristocratic faces. Artists whose work recorded the look of the day include Jean-Antoine Watteau, François Boucher, Thomas Gainsborough, and Sir Joshua Reynolds. It was also a time of new ways of thinking and living. Acquiring the correct posture and deportment could raise a person in status and class. As never before, it was possible to move up the social ladder out of a lower birth station through hard work, good looks, and finding the right dance and deportment teacher.

Recommended plays: By Molière, *Tartuffe;* by Oliver Goldsmith, *She Stoops to Conquer;* by John Gay, *The Beggar's Opera;* by Richard Sheridan, *The Rivals;* by Peter Shaffer, *Amadeus.*

RESTORATION/EIGHTEENTH-CENTURY SCHEMATIC, MALE

RESTORATION/EIGHTEENTH-CENTURY MAKEUP, MALE

RESTORATION/EIGHTEENTH-
CENTURY SCHEMATIC, FEMALE

RESTORATION/EIGHTEENTH-
CENTURY MAKEUP, FEMALE

EDWARDIAN

Because so many significant plays are set in the late Victorian and Edwardian period, around the turn of the twentieth century, a study of makeup for that era is important. But actually, a woman of quality living during that time would hardly have worn cosmetics; facial adornment was reserved for prostitutes. Of course, to achieve this "no makeup" look onstage, indeed one must wear makeup that simulates the Edwardian lady's fair skin, always protected by a hat, and her large, doelike eyes showing a little shading on the lids to accentuate their shape. Perhaps she puffed on white rice powder ever so lightly, and showed just a hint of color in her cheeks. As captured by artists of the day—notably John Singer Sargent, Charles Dana Gibson, Thomas Eakins, and Maxfield Parish—her face was round or oval and revealed no lines or wrinkles, as though she hadn't a care in the world. She was often depicted with the body of a woman and the face of a child. The ideal man, on the other hand, had a mature look—a face that showed fine lines and creases. In men, structure and strength were important, just as they were in the clothing, home furnishings, and building styles of the day.

Recommended plays: By George Bernard Shaw, *Major Barbara, Man and Superman, Pygmalion;* by James M. Barrie, *Peter Pan;* by Anton Chekhov, *The Three Sisters, The Cherry Orchard;* by Oscar Wilde, *The Importance of Being Earnest;* by Eugene O'Neill, *Ah, Wilderness!*

EDWARDIAN SCHEMATIC, MALE

EDWARDIAN MAKEUP, MALE

EDWARDIAN SCHEMATIC, FEMALE

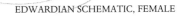

EDWARDIAN MAKEUP, FEMALE

JAZZ AGE

The 1920s mark the beginning of what we know today as modern times and the first youth movement. Women threw away their corsets, men their three-piece suits and stiff collars, and everyone had a very good time. Makeup for women was back in vogue. Bow-shaped lips, kohl-lined eyes, and long, dreamy eyelashes were musts for flappers. Men were clean-shaven, their hair center-parted, their look youthful and high-spirited.

Recommended plays: by Noel Coward, *Hay Fever, Bitter Sweet;* by Philip Barry, *Holiday;* by August Wilson, *Ma Rainey's Black Bottom;* by Luigi Pirandello, *Six Characters in Search of an Author.*

JAZZ AGE SCHEMATIC, MALE

JAZZ AGE MAKEUP, MALE

JAZZ AGE SCHEMATIC, FEMALE

JAZZ AGE MAKEUP, FEMALE

CHAPTER 11

stylization

ANY ORGANIC FORM can be stylized, from animal and human faces to plants and other products of nature. In Japan, Kabuki theater features some of the most exciting stylized makeup ever created, each face representing a type of character or an emotion. To a lesser extent, American musical theater uses stylization in costumes and makeup to clearly distinguish the hero from the "heavy." Consider the differences between good-guy Curly and bad-guy Judd in *Oklahoma!* or Jesus and Judas in *Jesus Christ Superstar.*

SIMPLIFY AND EXAGGERATE

I believe that your best approach to stylization is by studying animals. Animals often personify simple emotions: the lion, fearlessness; the mouse, timidity; the monkey, curiosity; the dog, faithfulness. If you scrutinize an animal's features and then simplify and exaggerate those forms, the result will be an exciting stylized makeup design.

Keep in mind that you don't have to use realistic colors for an animal stylization. In fact, your makeup design may be much more effective if you exaggerate your color scheme along with your facial features.

CHOOSE AN ANIMAL, CREATE A SKETCH

Select an animal to inspire you. Your reference should be a close-up photo of the animal's face, showing details of its features. You may choose from the animals presented here or find your own. Some animals lend themselves better to stylization than others. Very good choices are both domestic and wild cats, dogs (except collies and others with long snouts), most rodents, rabbits, owls, raccoons, pandas, koalas, monkeys, and apes. Difficult animals to stylize are those with projecting noses or eyes on the sides of their heads. For your first stylized project don't choose horses, bears, cows, pigs, elephants, giraffes, most reptiles, fish, and birds. Although I have seen some successful stylizations of fish, eagles, and bears, I don't recommend working with such animals until you are more experienced with this design genre.

Felines, such as this Sumatran tiger, are good choices for stylization.

Trace your animal's essential features from the photo. This tracing becomes the basis on which to build your stylization schematic.

OBSERVE THE EYE-NOSE-MOUTH CONNECTION

In building a schematic for your stylization makeup design, note that all animals have what I call an "eye-nose-mouth connection." Any animal that you work with will reveal this "face patch" pattern, although in different proportions according to species. Whenever you design animal makeup, refer to the drawings below to remind you of these connections among facial features.

DOG

CAT

RABBIT

MONKEY

Step 1. To create an animal stylization makeup design, on a clear photograph, outline the essential features of the animal's face, then transfer and embellish those lines on your Face Shape Schematic. Compare this line drawing with the one of the tiger on page 95.

Step 2. Developing the penciled Face Shape Schematic shown earlier (page 95), now establish colors for your tiger makeup design. Remember to simplify and exaggerate features, particularly by enlarging the eyes and mouth so that these most expressive parts of your onstage face will be clearly visible to the audience.

Step 3. Use eyeliner pencil to begin your makeup application. Draw lines that follow the overall pattern worked out on your schematic. These lines create a "face patch"—the focused area of interest that defines the animal. Note that the "eye-mouth-nose connection" is very clearly defined at this point.

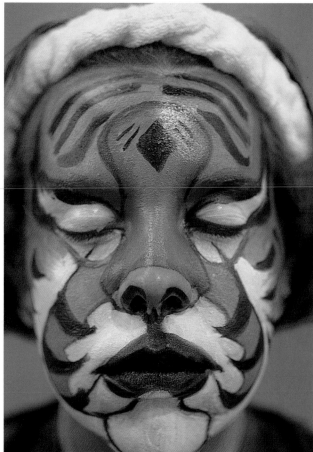

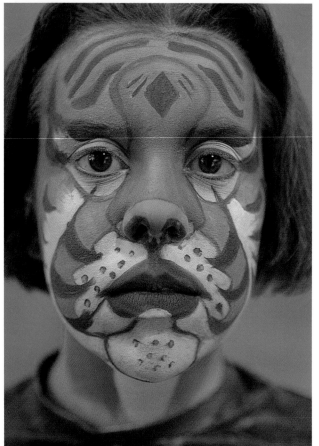

Step 4. When white makeup is part of your design scheme, put it on first, before applying foundation or other colors. This will prevent mixing of tones that would muddy the final look. Pat on white cream liner or clown white foundation with a sponge or brush, being careful to work between the lines without obliterating them. The next colors applied here are orange and brown foundation.

Step 5. Use contrasting colors and shading to create a more three-dimensional look, and remember to continue the makeup down to your neck to meet your costume. After painting your eye area, close your eyes and powder the lids immediately to keep the makeup from smudging. (It may help to have an assistant at this point, or work in pairs with another actor or student.)

Step 6. Finish applying makeup outside the "face patch," adding dots around the mouth to create a more feline effect.

Step 7. Check to see how your makeup looks when your face is animated, and add final touches accordingly. Use a neutral white powder to set makeup.

Kate Walker emphasized the nose and mouth area for her cheetah, created believable feline spots, and made up her neck to lengthen it.

Miranda Crispin lowered her forehead to force her cheetah's eyes-nose-mouth closer together, particularly emphasizing the mouth and eyes.

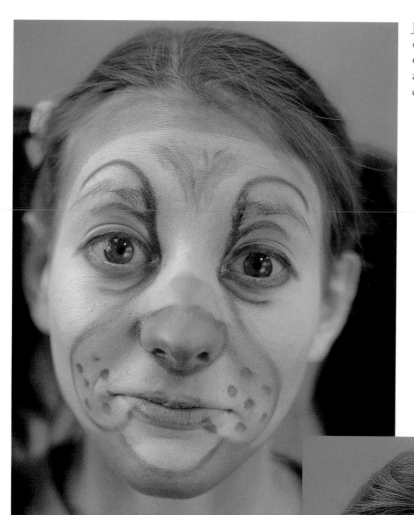

Jordyn Frelk created dog eyes successfully by overemphasizing eyebrows and bags to impart a sad, canine expression.

Stacey Wooden made good use of the eye-nose-mouth connection to create a cat. Notice how she uses her eyebrows as part of the overall design.

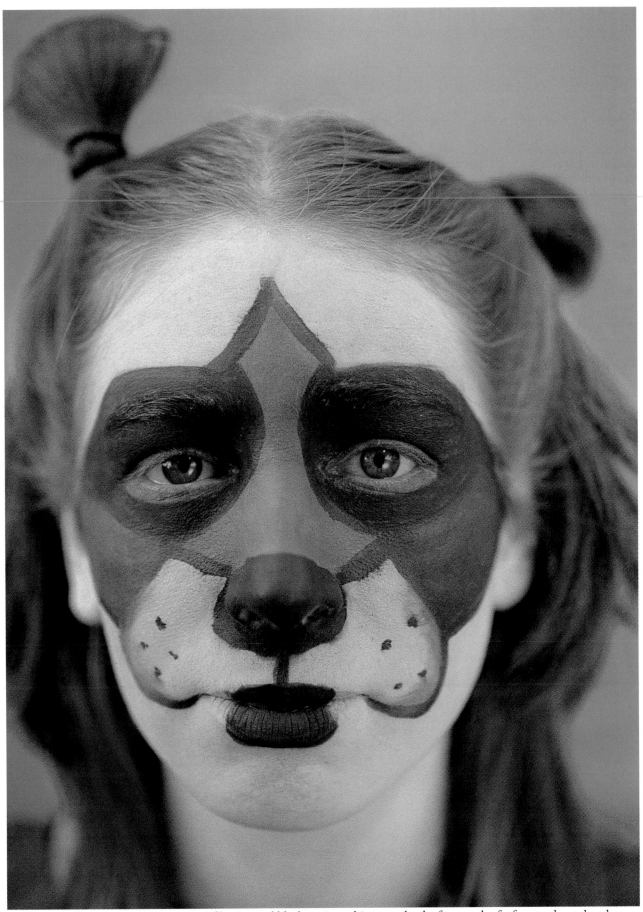

Catherine Hoban used strong contrasts of brown and black against white to make the face patch of a fox stand out sharply.

This lion schematic combines bold lines, exaggerated colors, and strong shapes to create a readily recognizable animal.

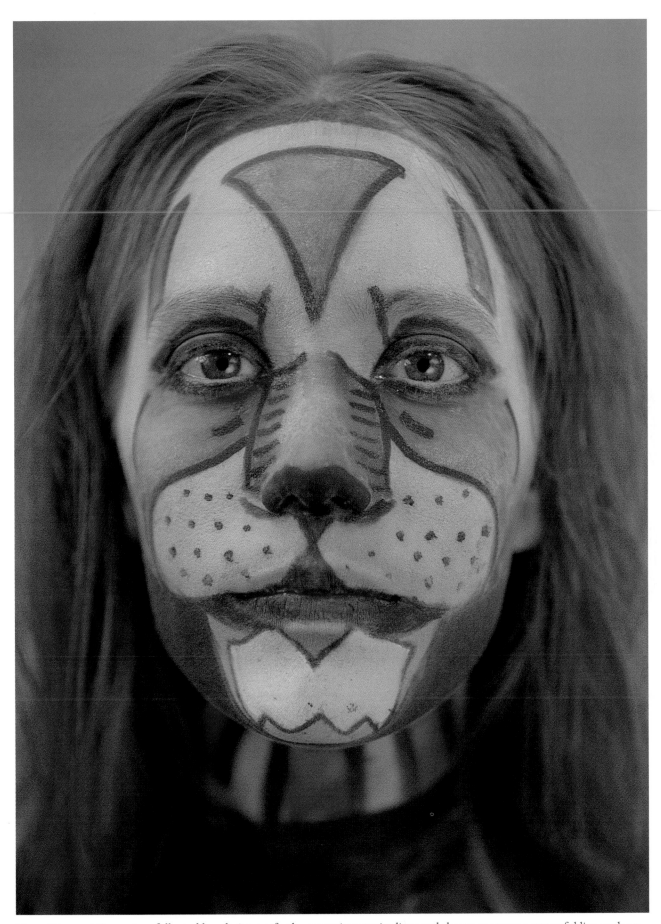

Here, Margaret Cummings followed her design perfectly, executing precise lines and shapes to create a powerful lion makeup.

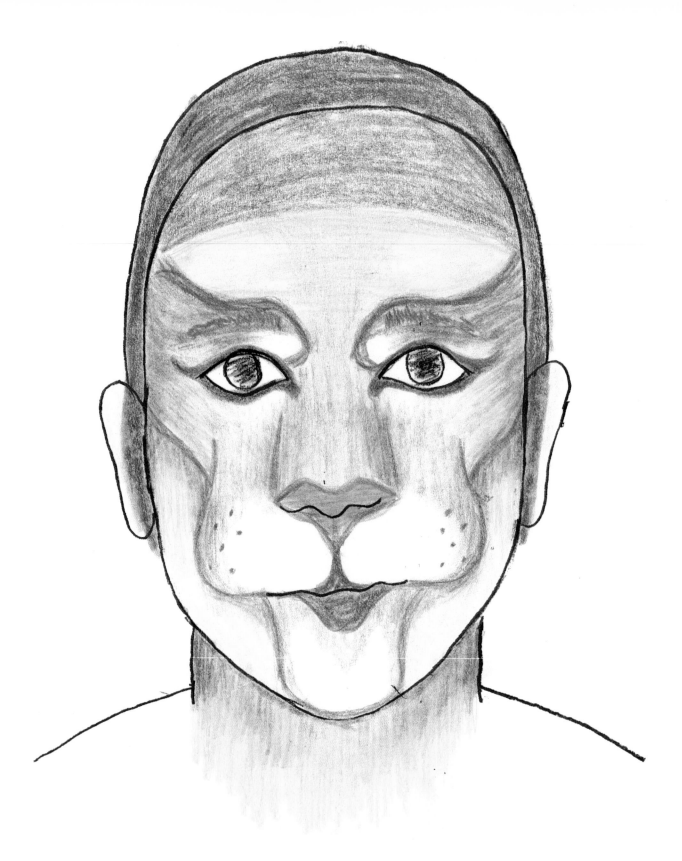

This lioness schematic has a soft, lyrical quality achieved
through harmonious colors, curving lines, and graceful shapes
that focus attention on the eyes, nose, and mouth areas.

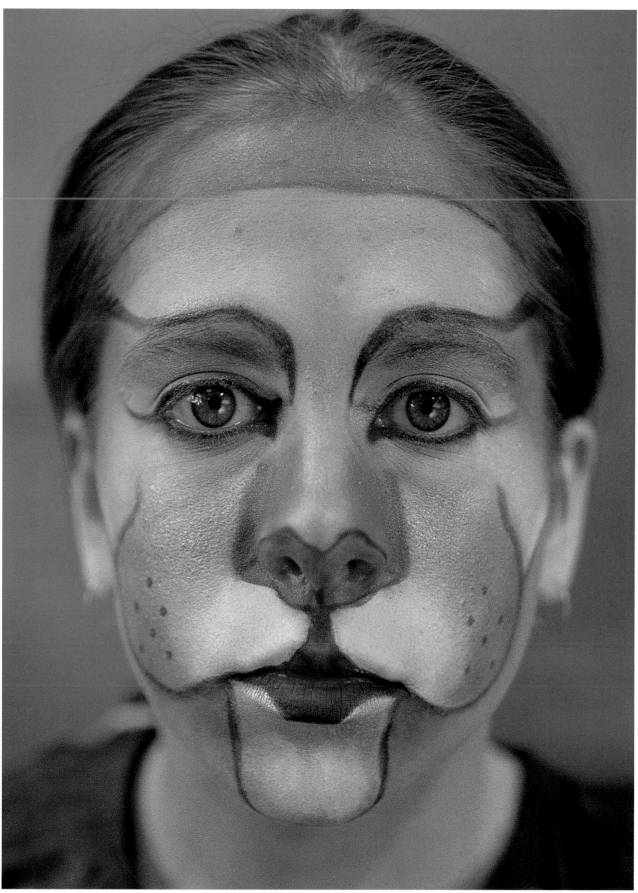

Kate Siepert used luminous makeup to create a bold lioness, following her schematic very faithfully while adjusting the cheeks to accommodate her natural contours.

CHAPTER 12

fantasy makeup

CREATING FANTASY MAKEUP is lots of fun.
It allows you to push your artistic imagination
beyond the limits of human facial features to
explore design motifs not normally considered for
use on the human face. These motifs might include
plant life and other organic forms; the seasons and
elements; images from famous paintings; patterns
based on household items and other familiar
objects; and numerous other sources that can be
abstracted and adapted to makeup concepts in
nontraditional ways, designed to create an emo-
tional impact on an audience while still evoking
a dramatic persona.

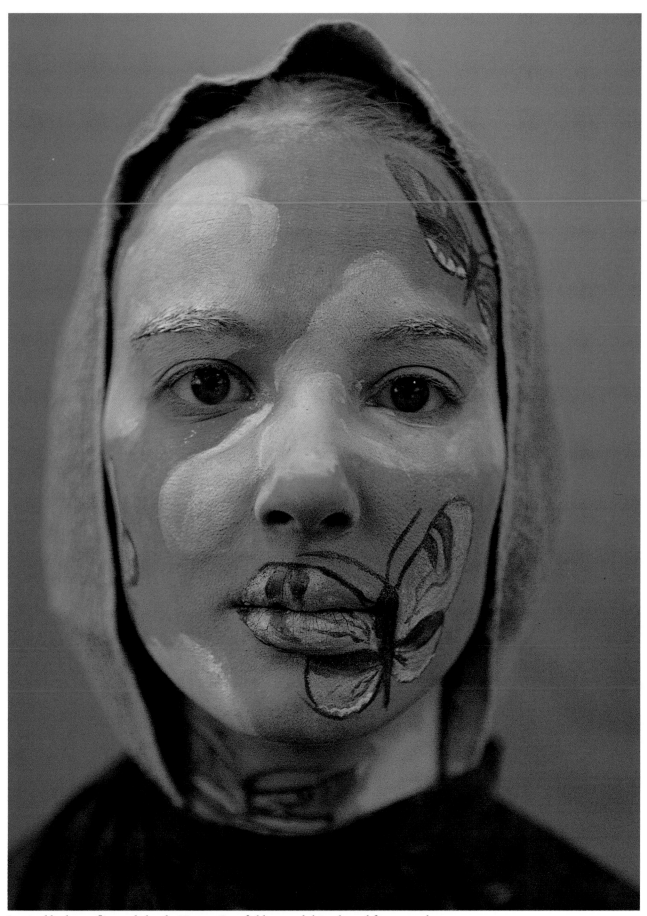

Inspired by butterflies and clouds, Kirsten Gronfield created this ethereal fantasy makeup.

SELECTING A FANTASY THEME

Pick a character from a play and make a list of about eight descriptive adjectives to define your role—for example: sunny, warm, pink, homey, cottony-soft, squishy, sugary, and light. Look for these characteristics in artwork, familiar advertisements, nature photos, and any other visual material that fits your list of adjectives. For the example I've cited, a match-up for my "sunny, warm, pink, etc." characteristics might be a painting by Pierre-Auguste Renoir.

Synthesize the information in the source that inspires you, and design makeup to represent it. In other words, create a face design that epitomizes the character you have chosen through the use of descriptive adjectives.

It's very important that you not use realistic colors. Don't apply natural skin tones; instead, experiment with colors that are not associated with the human face in its realistic form.

It's also important to camouflage, obliterate, or ignore your own facial features as much as possible for this design project, or to exaggerate them in an extreme way.

The challenge is to keep your design simple enough to be read from an audience perspective. This can be best accomplished by not putting too much information on your face.

SOURCES OF INSPIRATION

When I gave this enjoyable assignment to my students, five chose famous paintings on which to base fantasy makeup, each taking advantage of powerful visual imagery of masterful artists to inspire them. Three students turned to nature for evocative themes, and one borrowed her idea from children's literature. I hope that these examples will stimulate equally imaginative fantasy makeup ideas of your own.

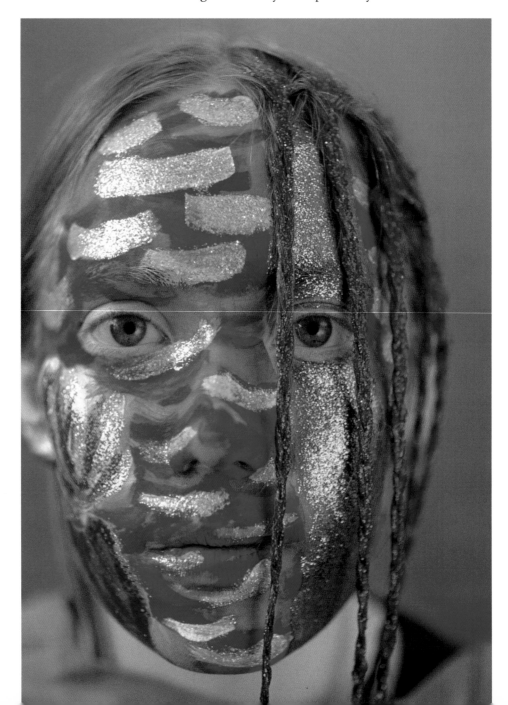

Margaret Cummings based her design on Claude Monet's famous water lily paintings. Contrasting cool blues and greens against warm reds and yellows, she adds highlights with glitter makeup liners used on her skin and on strands of hair smartly integrated into her design.

SUNFLOWER SCHEMATIC

Miranda Crispin's yellow sunflower petals, brightened further by flecks of white, pop forward against a field of greens. By making her brushstrokes visible, she adds texture and dimension to her design.

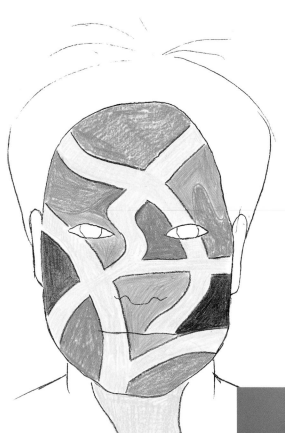

STORYBOOK SCHEMATIC

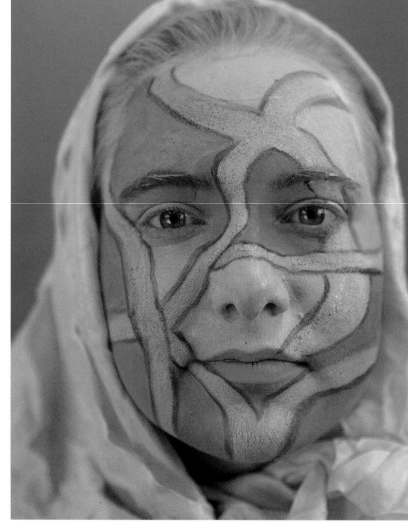

Laura-Kate Burleson was inspired by *Oh, the Places You Will Go,* a beloved Dr. Seuss children's book, cleverly represented by a labyrinth of roads and bright fields.

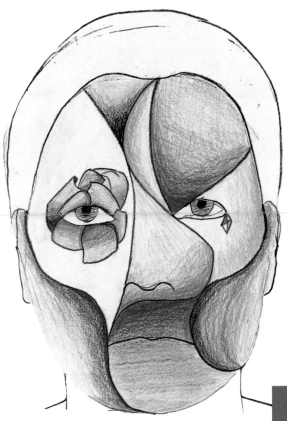

PICASSO SCHEMATIC

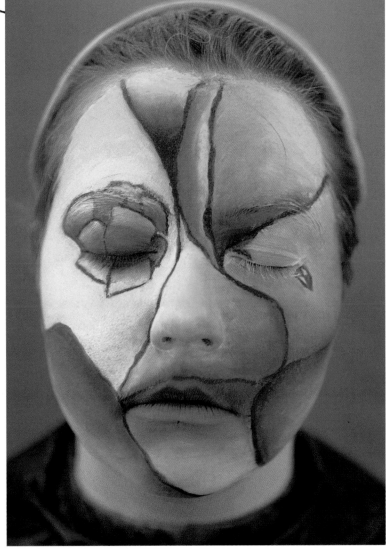

Kerissa Ward blends shades of blue, white, and purple in a painterly fashion, creating a sectioned pattern that is reminiscent of Pablo Picasso's lively cubist period.

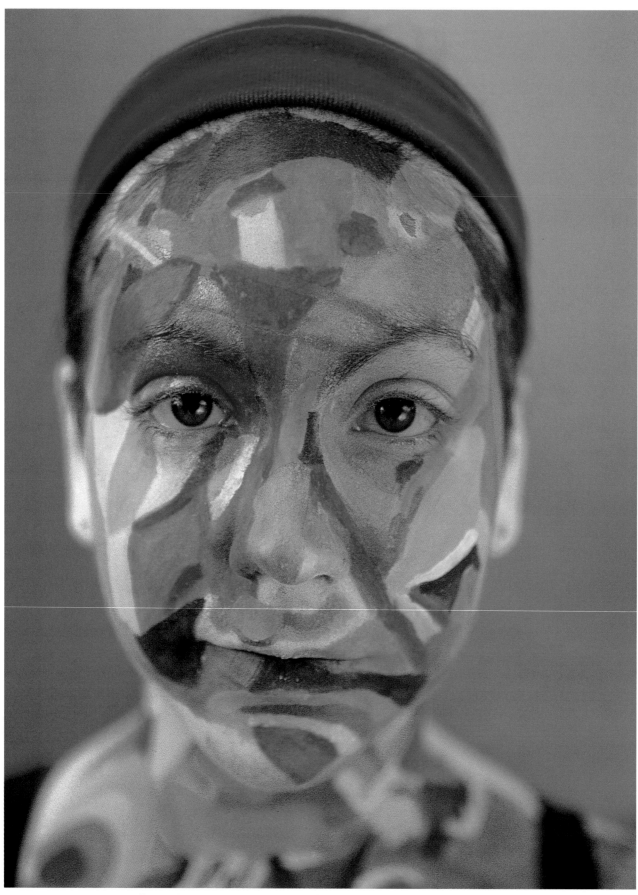

Jamie Zauner captures the flavor of Wassily Kandinsky's expressionist paintings with this wildly colorful abstraction painted on both face and neck.

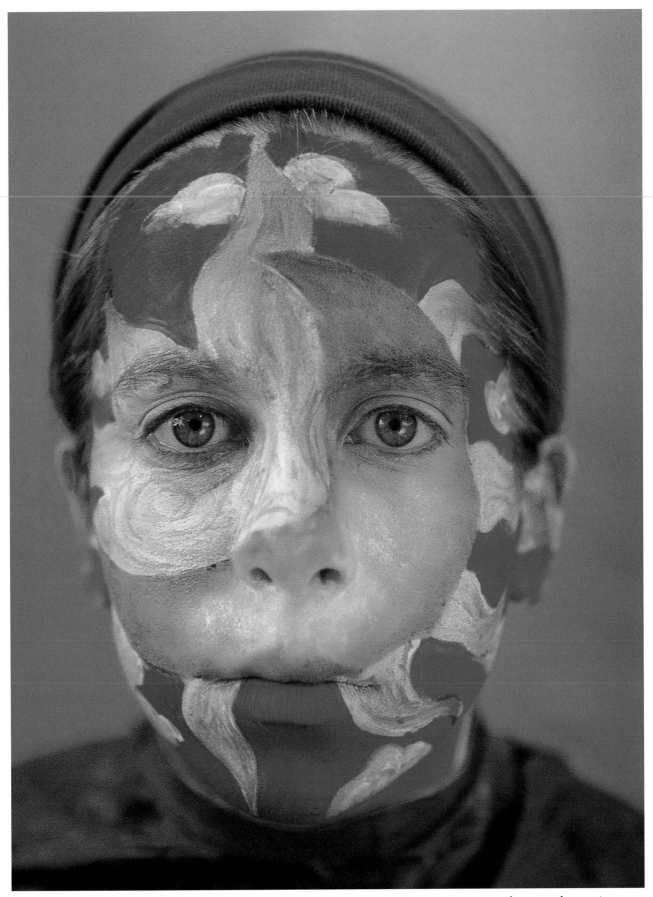

Kate Siepert combines a fiery yellow-orange-red palette with cool blue-gray-white tones to portray the sun and moon in a cloudy sky.

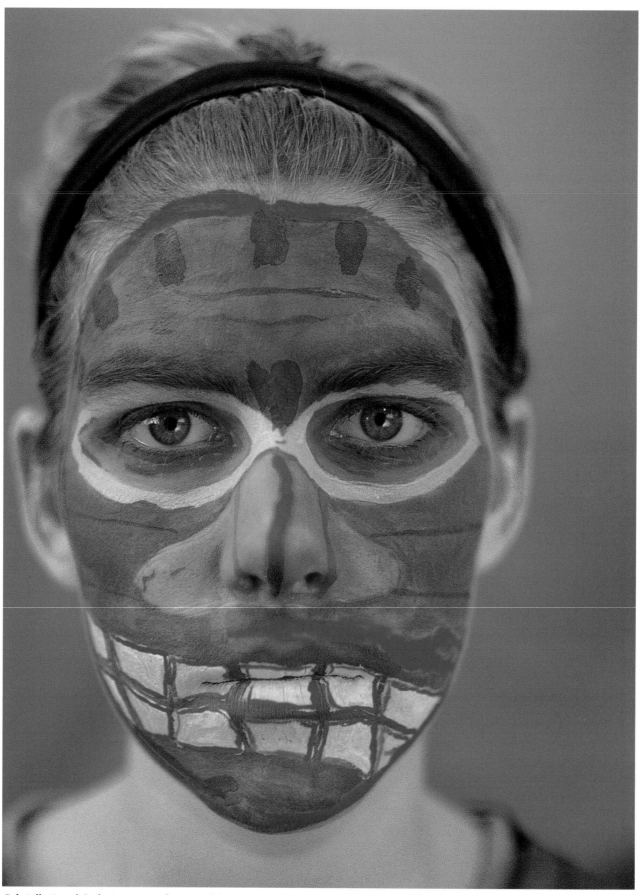

Gabrielle Rysula's design comes from work by contemporary painter Jean-Michel Basquiat, whose forceful abstract images are faithfully represented by both strong pattern and color.

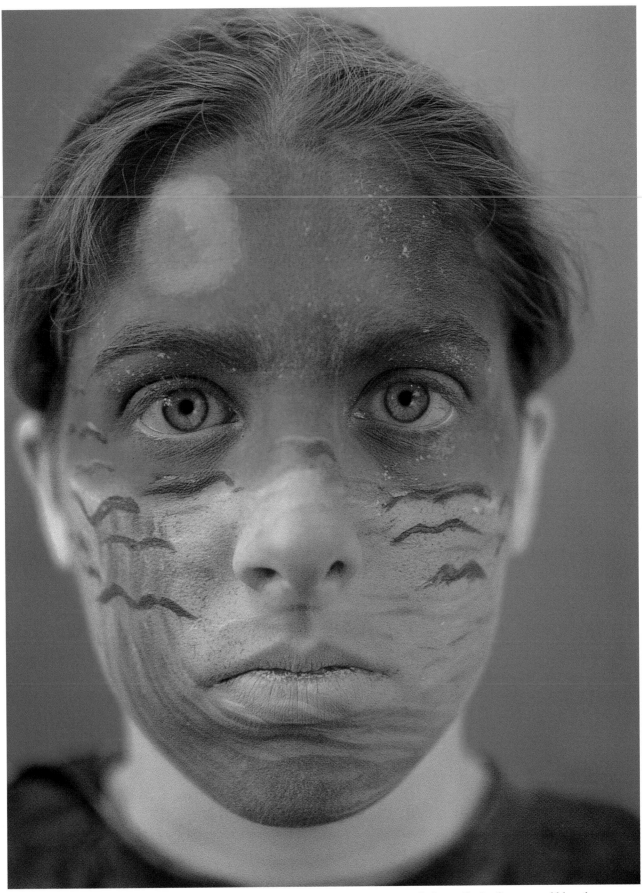

Nicole Hand's evocative interpretation of a famous Vincent van Gogh painting includes its flock of crows and blue sky over a golden wheat field.

CHAPTER 13

UPON OCCASION, an actor will be asked
to play a character of the opposite gender.
Theater history has many wonderful examples
of women playing men and men playing women,
most often in comedies where the roles present
actors with many delightful challenges—the first
one being how to change facial features to create
a masculine or feminine look.

ANALYZING MALE AND FEMALE FEATURES

Before attempting to make a male face look female or vice versa, think about the general difference in the structure of men's and women's faces.

Eyebrows are usually heavier and closer to the eyes on men; women's eyebrows are thinner, more shaped, higher above the eyes.

Men's noses are often wider and more bulbous than women's; finer, straighter lines and smaller nostrils often characterize women's noses.

Thinner lips and a more pronounced jawline and chin are associated with male faces; fuller lips, a softer jawline, and smaller chin are associated with female faces.

Observe how all these differences are dealt with in the two exercises of makeup designs that follow.

Schematics that transform a man's face into a woman's or a woman's face into a man's should be fully detailed, including hair design, before beginning your makeup application.

EXERCISE MAKING A MALE LOOK FEMALE

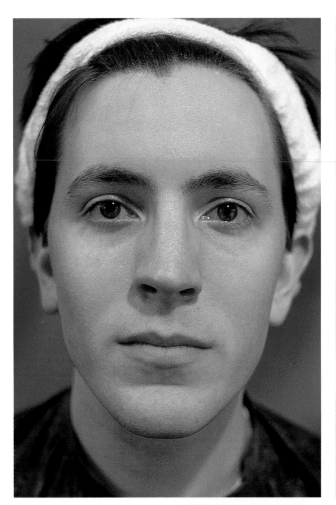

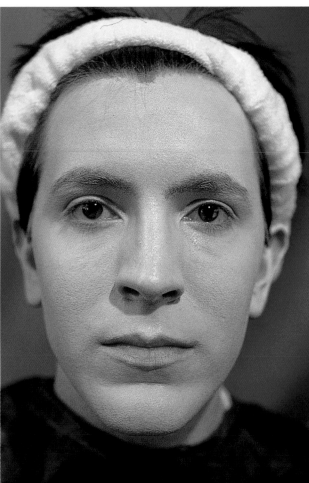

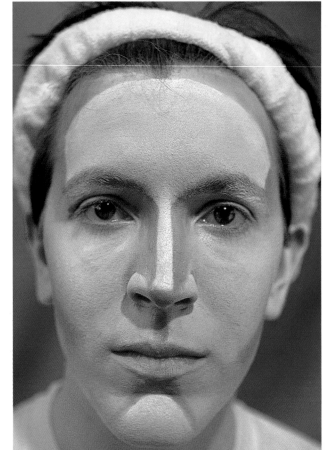

Step 1. Look at our model's face without makeup. Based on the guidelines given above, which areas of his face would you say need the most makeup application to give him a convincing female look?

Step 2. Choose a foundation that controls ruddiness and gives you a peachy glow (Mehron's Fair Female and Soft Peach foundations are used here); apply it evenly out into your hairline. Be careful to get good coverage around your eyes and nose.

Step 3. Apply basic highlight and shadow lines to round and lower your forehead, narrow and straighten your nose, reduce your nostril size, open up your eyes, lift your cheekbones, and shape your chin. Remember to powder after all the contouring is completed.

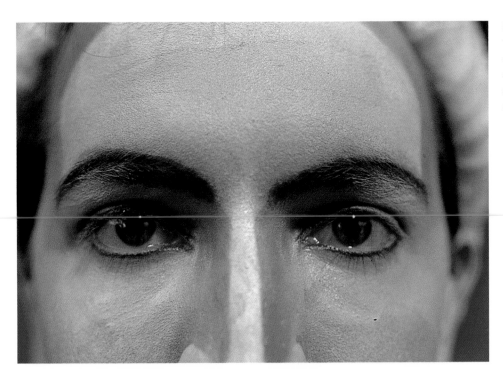

Step 4. Use an eyeliner in a warm brown tone to round and pull your eyes a bit closer together and to raise and shape your eyebrows into arches.

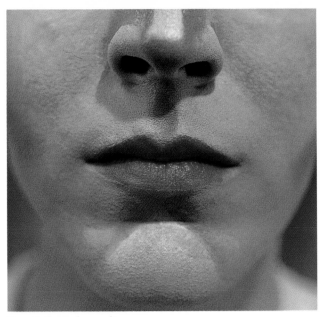

Step 5. Round your lips with a liner pencil to create a more feminine, bowlike shape. Don't overexaggerate lip size.

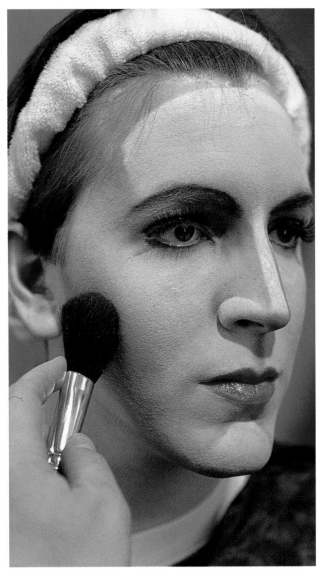

Step 6. Place blush higher on your cheeks than your would for male stage makeup. Add false eyelashes and gray eye shadow.

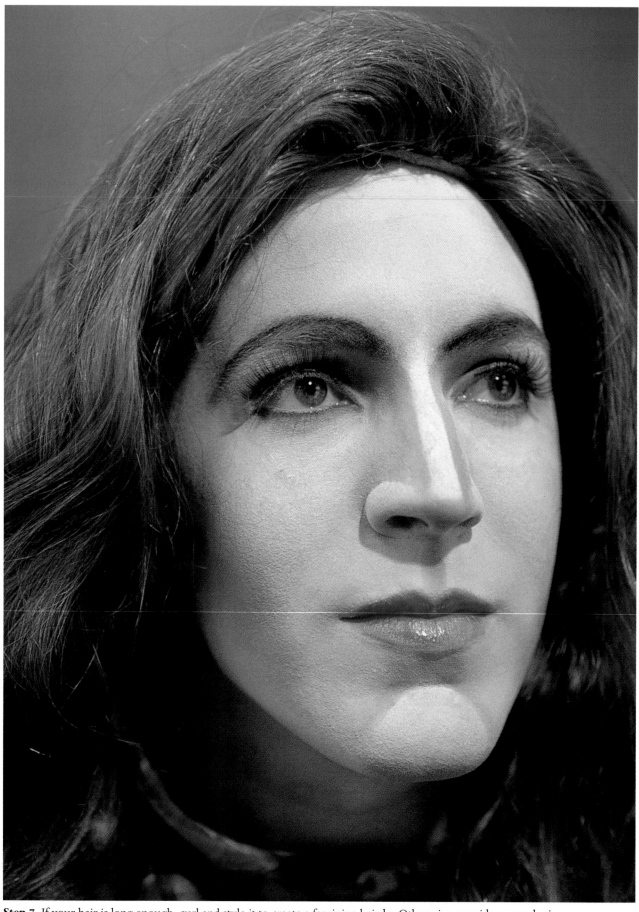

Step 7. If your hair is long enough, curl and style it to create a feminine hairdo. Otherwise, consider a good wig.

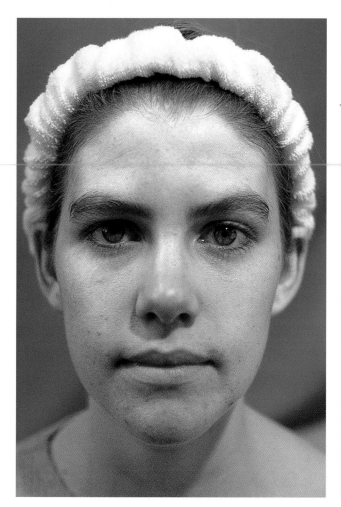

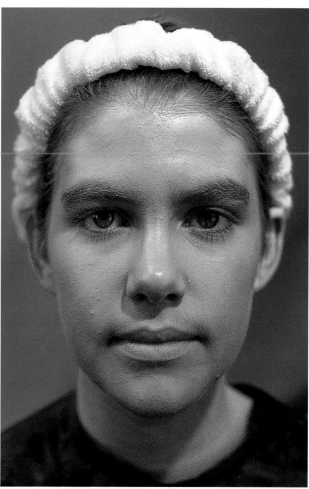

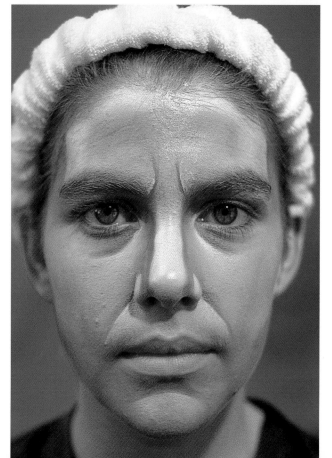

Step 1. Look at our model's face without makeup. Based on the guidelines given earlier, which areas of her face would you say need the most makeup application to give her a convincing male look?

Step 2. Choose a foundation that darkens and bronzes your skin slightly (Mehron's Medium Male and Ben Nye's Naturelle Buff are used here), and apply it evenly out into your hairline.

Step 3. Use highlight and shadow liners to broaden and square your forehead, paint creases between your eyebrows and slight bags under your eyes, widen your nose, square your jawline and chin, and emphasize your nasolabial folds. Remember to powder after all the contouring is completed.

Step 4. Using a medium-brown pencil liner, increase the width and fullness of your eyebrows, and lightly outline the corners or your eyes to pull them farther apart.

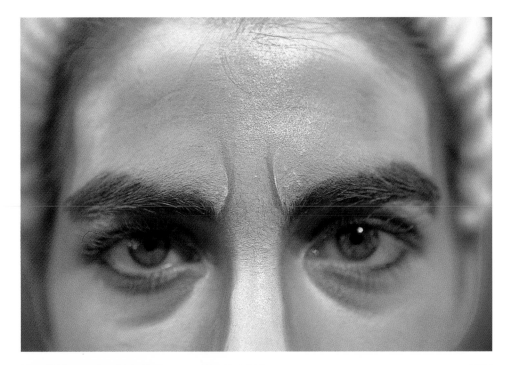

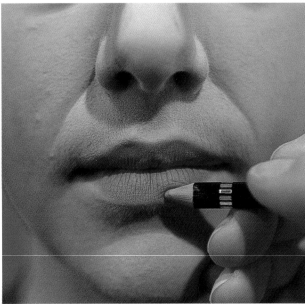

Step 5. Reduce the roundness inherent in many female lips by lightly lining your mouth, decreasing the upper lip bow and reducing the fullness of the lower lip.

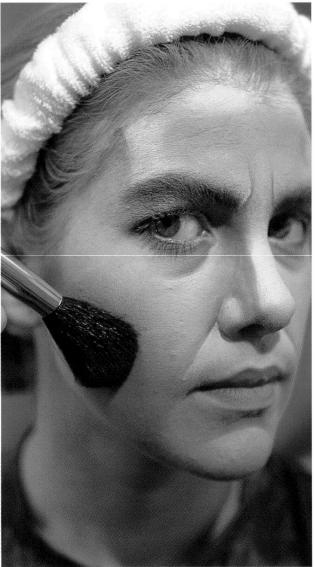

Step 6. Lower your cheekbones with highlight, and rouge below the bone, using a bronze-tone blusher in the hollow of the cheek.

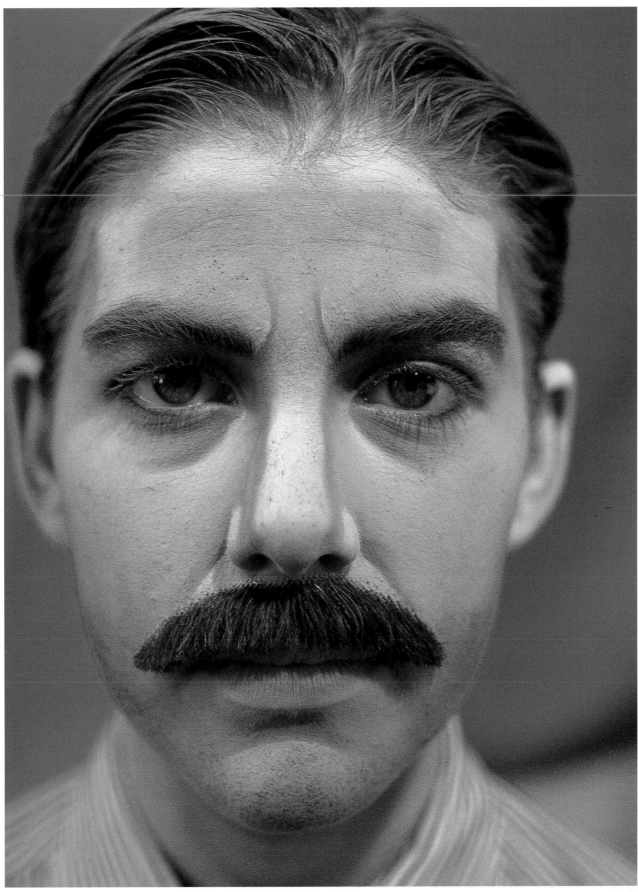

Step 7. A mustache and stippling on the jaw and chin contribute to this convincing gender reversal, and the model's hair is gelled and styled to look masculine. If you have long hair, it may be pulled back into a male-style ponytail or concealed under a wig.

facial hair, hairpieces, and wigs

THE FINAL STEP in completing a stage makeup often entails adding a mustache, a beard, a supplementary hairpiece, or a full wig. This chapter covers the basics in each category.

For beards, there are two distinct types. A ventilated beard—much more durable than a crepe-hair beard— is hand crafted from human hair onto lace to look exactly like the real thing and will last, with care, for years to come. For most theatrical productions it is the best choice. However, crepe hair, or crepe wool, is sometimes used for smaller facial hairpieces.

USING CREPE WOOL FOR FACIAL HAIR

Crepe wool (or crepe hair) is a quick, realistic-looking product for creating a mustache, a van dyke, and even a beard. But it's not a replacement for ventilated hairpieces, which are preferred by most actors for their durability and believability. However, crepe wool can be simple to apply, effective, and considerably less expensive a choice when needed for a single performance or other limited usage.

Crepe wool comes in various shades of blond, brunette, black, auburn, gray, and white. With many preblended shades offered, custom blending is rarely needed. Crepe wool also comes in bright colors for fantasy applications.

When designing facial hair, first consider the type of mustache or beard that best serves your role. Decide if your facial hair should be the same color as the hair (or wig) on your head; often facial hair doesn't match head hair exactly. Also take into account how reusable the piece must be and how much time you can devote to building (and possibly rebuilding) it for each performance.

Crepe wool comes from the manufacturer as a thick, tight braid around a long jute cord. First, you cut off the length you need: about four inches for a full mustache; six to ten inches for a beard. Then you pull and unravel the wool fiber. Since it's quite wavy from having been braided, if you want your facial hairpiece to be free of waves, straighten it with a steam iron. Simply lay the cut section of hair—slightly separated, no longer in a hard braid—on an ironing board (atop a cloth to protect the board's cover from hairs). Use a fairly hot iron, and since it helps to dampen the hair, use the steam setting. Hold one end of the separated braid as you iron the other end, slightly tugging at the braid to help straighten fibers, then turn the hair around and press the other end, continue the process until you have the desired straightness.

Photograph by Scott Kemmerer

For durability, use a beard and mustache in ventilated styles with the quality of hair matched to your own hair, as shown here.

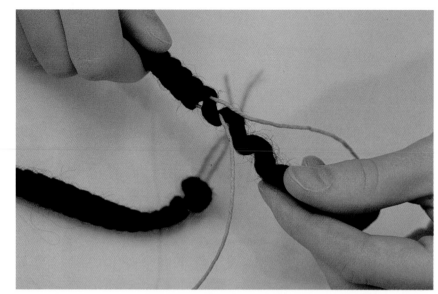

Step 1. To create a moderate-size, two-piece mustache, cut a four-inch length of crepe wool and begin opening the braid.

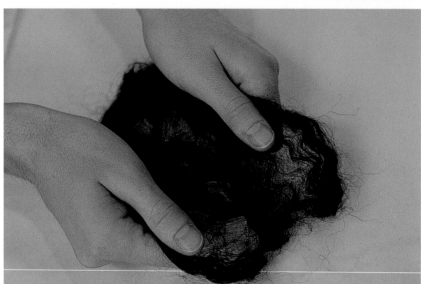

Step 2. Separate the fibers by tugging at them with both hands. To straighten them more, use a steam iron.

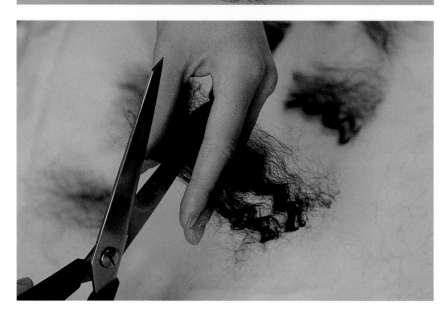

Step 3. Once the fibers are straight, separate the hank into smaller sections. A mustache needs at least four to six layers of hair to look real. Leave the sections longer than you want the finished piece to be; you can trim it to fit your face after constructing it.

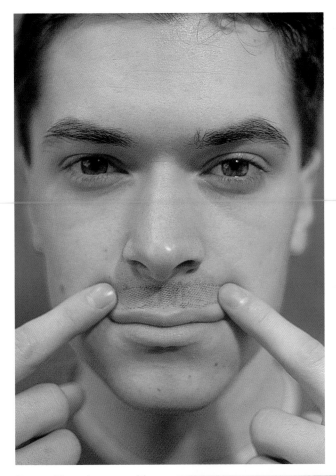

Step 4. To make a reusable crepe mustache, build it on tulle (a lightweight netting sold at fabric and craft stores). Shape and cut the tulle to the general size of the mustache base by outlining its shape with a pencil liner. Then trim and hold the net on your face to check its fit. (Notice that I drew two sections with a separation at the center.)

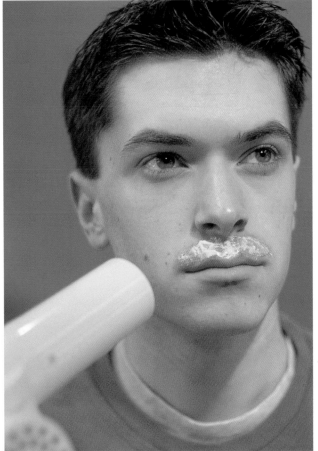

Step 5. Using clear liquid latex, paint the mustache area, embed the tulle into it, then paint another thin layer of latex over the tulle to secure it tightly.

Step 6. Use a hair dryer on a medium setting to speed up drying time so the tulle will be ready to receive layers of crepe wool.

Step 7. To build your mustache, introduce the crepe hair into the latex layer by layer. Get an even edge on each layer by trimming it into a straight line, then paint a fine line of latex at the bottom of the tulle and press the hairs into the latex at a 90-degree angle to the face, as shown. Repeat this process, moving upward until you have the desired look and thickness. Don't flatten the hairs or press downward at any time or the hairs will look messy and latex will show through. It's important to work quickly because latex dries fast, especially under your nose!

Step 8. While the mustache is still in place, trim it into the right shape. If some latex still shows as white, use spirit gum to apply a small amount of hair to cover the area. However, remember that even a small spot of latex won't be visible to the audience from stage.

Step 9. Remove the mustache from your face by gently pulling the tulle from its outside edge. The whole mustache should come off in one piece. Trim it further if necessary.

Step 10. Reapply the mustache with spirit gum. Stretch your face by smiling, to see that glue has secured the mustache fully. Notice that the piece has now been trimmed, shaped, and split into two halves, and that no part of the tulle base shows.

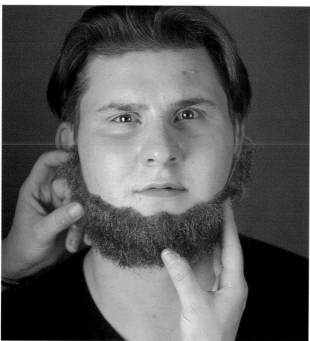

Step 1. To see how it will fit, put the beard against your face (or have a partner help you). Needed adjustments may be trimming the lace to fit your face shape or to fade the hair into your sideburns; sewing a dart into the lace to reshape the beard for a narrow face; or releasing a dart already there to adjust for a larger jaw.

Step 2. Trim the lace on the back of the beard. To keep it in place while trimming, the chin section of the beard is attached lightly to the face with toupee tape. When you remove the tape, before affixing the beard, make sure your face is clean and dry; always apply makeup after a facial hairpiece is glued down.

Step 3. After removing the toupee tape, apply a light coating of water-soluble spirit gum to your face where the beard will be attached; apply spirit gum to the beard as well. Allow both gummed areas to dry until tacky to the touch, then begin application in the chin area, working out to each side.

Step 4. At the outer edges of the beard near your sideburns, use toupee tape instead of spirit gum, which can easily get on sideburns. The white paper peels off the toupee tape, leaving double-sided tape to hold down loose edges. Stretch your face by smiling, to see that glue has secured the beard fully.

Step 5. Finish by applying a coordinated mustache and a few hairs under your lower lip to create a full-bearded look.

HAIRPIECE ENHANCEMENTS

Sometimes enhancing your own hair with an artificial hairpiece is preferable to donning a full wig for a particular role. Supplemental hairpieces are especially useful for transforming short hair into long, or making thin hair appear thicker so that it can be styled into hairdos ranging from the formal and the bouffant to the wild and windblown.

EXERCISE ADDING A FALL

Step 1. Brush the hair on the crown of your head upward, and holding it there, attach a "banana clip" fall—a ponytail, or thick hank of hair, mounted on a clip.

Step 2. Secure and close the clip to join the fall to your own hair. This addition will enhance short hair, or even shoulder-length hair, by giving it extra body and height.

Step 3. Comb your own hair that comes over the top of the clip and blend it in with the fall. Spray to style and shape your hair into a full and natural-looking cascade.

Step 1. Form curls on the crown of your head, using two bobby pins per curl.

Step 2. Section your hair from the sides of your head and begin twisting and wrapping strands, then pinning them in place.

Step 3. Finish wrapping and pinning your hair until it is all pinned very close to your scalp. Be sure that there are no stray, unsecured strands of hair.

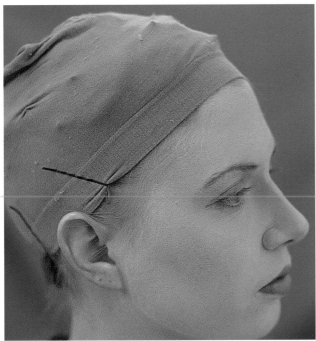

Step 4. Use the panty part of pantyhose (legs cut off and sewn shut) as a wig cap, and pin it in place. (Commercial wig caps are available but are often too small for larger heads.)

Step 5. Place the front of the wig at the top of your forehead, just at the edge of your wig cap.

Step 6. After pulling the wig down in back, anchor it to your wig cap with bobby pins: one through the wig at the crown, one at each side of the nape of your neck, and one pin at each ear. Bring some hair forward to create a more natural hairline. (If your hair is the same color as the wig, release a few strands of your own hair onto your forehead.)

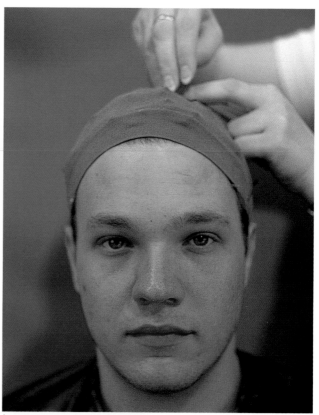

Step 1. If your hair is long enough, it should be pin-curled in place on the crown of your head before putting the wig cap over it. Then place the wig cap at the top of your forehead and pull up and over the pin curls.

Step 2. Once the cap is in place, pin through it at the top and sides to secure it firmly. Now the wig has a strong anchor base.

Step 3. Place the front of the wig at the top of your fore-head, then pull it up and over the cap, down to the nape of your neck.

Step 4. Once the wig is in place, pin at each ear, on both sides of the nape of your neck, and at the crown of the wig right through the wig cap for total security.

making a life mask

AT SOME POINT, you may find it useful to have a life mask of your face as a base on which to experiment with casting prosthetics—new facial shapes, such as a false nose, made out of latex and foam. (As noted earlier, actual prosthetic construction is beyond the scope of this book.) This chapter will show you how to create your life mask. Since it's impossible to cast your own life mask because it's molded right on your face, find a partner to work with—ideally, another actor with whom you can make a reciprocal arrangement. Be careful not to choose anyone who's claustrophobia prone, as this process requires the subject's face to be covered for up to an hour.

PREPARATION AND MATERIALS NEEDED

Sit in a comfortable chair in a room that has plenty of light and running tap water. Tune in some relaxing music. Wear a plastic apron to protect your clothing totally (I use trash bags over a hair stylist's cape secured in place with masking tape), and a wig cap or wide headband that pulls all hair away from your face. Since your mouth will be covered and you won't be able to speak to your partner once the materials are plastered on your face, hand signals will be very comforting and necessary for communication, so work them out in advance. Your eyes will be also be closed tightly for some time, so your partner should reassure you that all's well by speaking calmly and frequently to you throughout the process.

MATERIALS

To make your life mask, assemble the following materials:

- trash bags to cover floor in working area

- plastic cape, trash bags, masking tape for model's protective covering

- wig cap or wide headband

- apron for partner's protective covering

- jar of petroleum jelly

- 1-pound bag of alginate: regular-set version sold by theatrical or dental supply houses; flavorless blend is preferable

- measuring cups (that come with alginate)

- mixing spoon

- tap water

- 4 plastic mixing bowls, about 10-ounce-size each

- 4 rubber spatulas, including 1 small

- plaster bandages, precut in varying lengths, available from medical supply, craft, or art stores, and a shallow pan of warm water

- hair dryer

- 1/2-gallon plaster of paris and plastic bowl to mix it in

- shallow pan with foam peanuts or sand for holding the mask as it dries

- paper towels

EXERCISE CREATING THE MASK

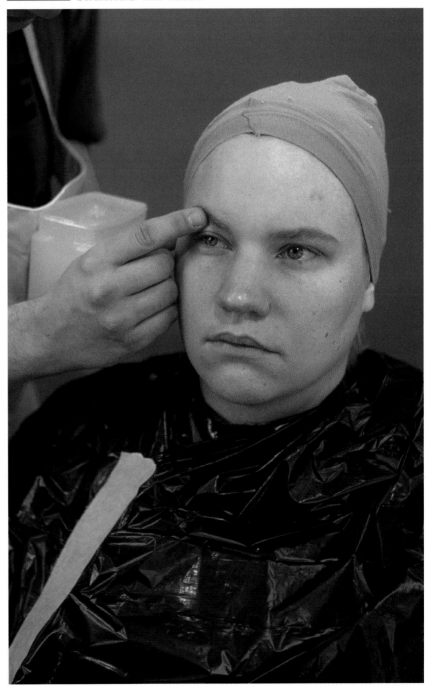

Step 1. Now to describe the active role, with you creating your partner's mask, begin by applying petroleum jelly to the eyebrows and eyelashes.

Step 2. Put alginate in each of four bowls, using the measuring cups provided. Pour water (1/2-cup water to 1/4-cup alginate) into the first bowl of alginate and stir until all dry powder is wet and has the consistency of thin pudding. Since alginate sets up within seconds when water is added, prepare only one bowl at a time, and work with it quickly. The water temperature also affects drying speed; the warmer the water, the quicker the set-up. (A retardant is also available that can be purchased with alginate.)

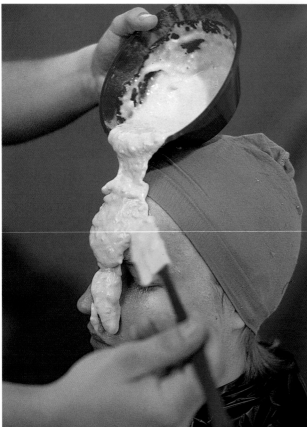

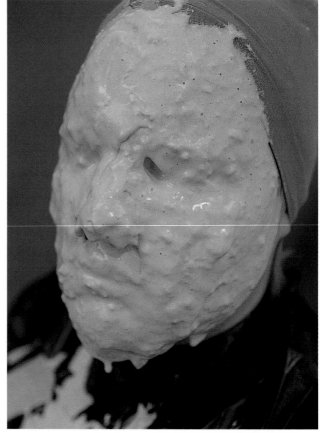

Step 3. Immediately pour alginate on the face, beginning at the top of the forehead. With a small spatula, press the mixture into the eye sockets firmly and evenly to prevent air pockets in the corners of the eyes. Since alginate dries quickly on spatulas, have clean ones ready to use as you proceed, one spatula for each bowl of mixture.

Step 4. With water added to the second bowl of alginate, then the third and fourth as you're ready to use them, continue pouring the mixture on the face. Cover the entire face and under the chin—but *make sure not to cover the nostrils*. If some alginate should get inside the nose, ask your partner to blow forcefully through the nostrils, which will enable you to remove the excess alginate as it is exhaled.

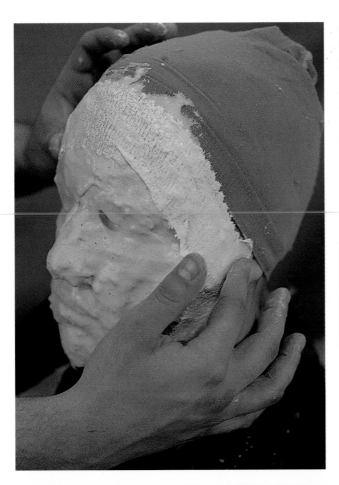

Step 5. Once the face is entirely covered with the alginate, wet precut plaster bandage strips and begin applying them across and down over the face. Use small strips to cover the nostril areas.

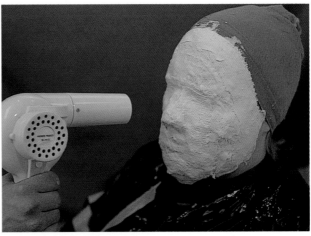

Step 6. Use a hair dryer on a moderate setting to speed up drying time of the plaster bandages. Always ask your partner if the dryer setting is at a comfortable level.

Step 7. Once the bandages are dry, by leaning forward with a scrunched-up face, your friend can help the alginate release from the undercuts (eye sockets, mouth) of the face. Also, in that position, gravity will aid in pulling off the mask. You will also need to run your finger around the mask between the edge of the alginate and your friend's skin to help release the mask from the wig cap, hairline, and chin.

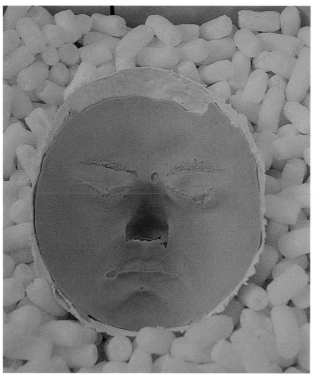

Step 8. Once the mask is off, cover the nose holes on the plaster side with small strips of plaster bandages and quickly dry that area with a blow dryer. Lay the mask in a shallow pan with packing peanuts for support. Fill the mask with wet paper towels (not shown) to slow drying time as you prepare plaster for the next step.

Step 9. Mix about four cups of plaster of paris with enough water to produce a smooth, puddinglike consistency, free of air bubbles.

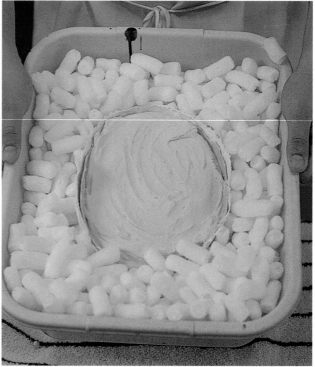

Step 10. After removing the paper towels from the mold, pour in a thin coating and press gently with your fingers to get the plaster into every crease and corner.

Step 11. Now fill the mold with plaster up to the brim. Be careful not to overfill. Allow the plaster to dry overnight, then remove and discard the alginate and plaster bandage mold and discard, leaving a perfect plaster life mask.

Step 12. The life mask held next to the model's face shows how accurate a likeness this process can produce.

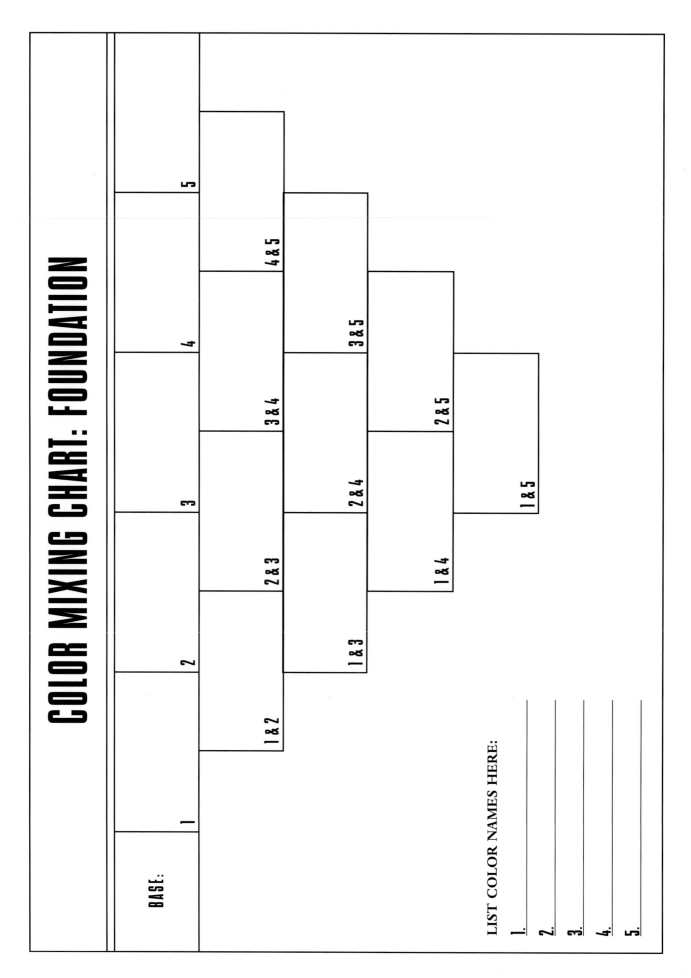

COLOR MIXING CHART: FOUNDATION

BASE:

| | 1 | 2 | 3 | 4 | 5 |

| 1 & 2 | 2 & 3 | 3 & 4 | 4 & 5 |

| 1 & 3 | 2 & 4 | 3 & 5 |

| 1 & 4 | 2 & 5 |

| 1 & 5 |

LIST COLOR NAMES HERE:

1. _____
2. _____
3. _____
4. _____
5. _____

COLOR MIXING CHART: FOUNDATION

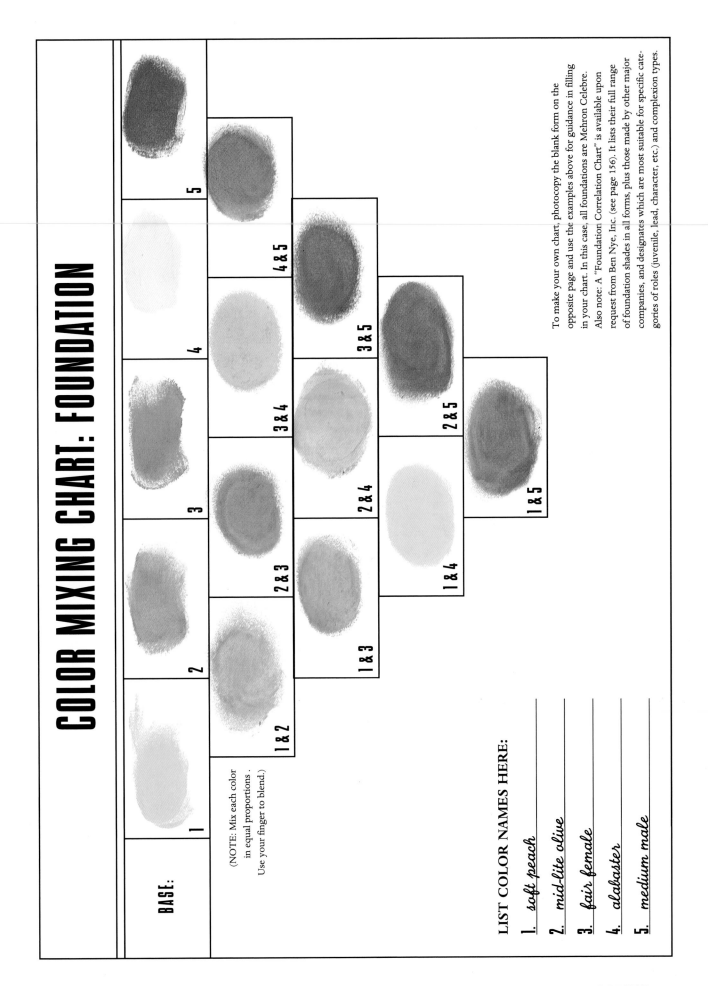

BASE:

| 1 | 2 | 3 | 4 | 5 |

(NOTE: Mix each color in equal proportions. Use your finger to blend.)

| 1 & 2 | 2 & 3 | 3 & 4 | 4 & 5 |

| 1 & 3 | 2 & 4 | 3 & 5 |

| 1 & 4 | 2 & 5 |

| 1 & 5 |

LIST COLOR NAMES HERE:

1. _soft peach_
2. _mid-lite olive_
3. _fair female_
4. _alabaster_
5. _medium male_

To make your own chart, photocopy the blank form on the opposite page and use the examples above for guidance in filling in your chart. In this case, all foundations are Mehron Celebre. Also note: A "Foundation Correlation Chart" is available upon request from Ben Nye, Inc. (see page 156). It lists their full range of foundation shades in all forms, plus those made by other major companies, and designates which are most suitable for specific categories of roles (juvenile, lead, character, etc.) and complexion types.

COLOR MIXING CHART: CREAM LINERS

WARM	
COOL	
TINTS	
SHADES	
HIGHLIGHTS	
SHADOWS	
EXPERIMENT!	

COLOR MIXING CHART: CREAM LINERS

WARM				
Mehron red lip rouge	Ben Nye maroon	Bob Kelly golden yellow	Bob Kelly bronze	

This sample chart shows how your own records might be kept. Simply photocopy the blank chart on the opposite page and fill in your own entries. My examples include liners by different manufacturers, which is how you should build your personal supply. Contact information for suppliers is on page 156.

COOL

Bob Kelly ocean blue   Bob Kelly shallow purple   Bob Kelly grey   Mehron jet black

(Optional)

TINTS

(Mix white with all warm and cools)

SHADES

(Mix black with all warm and cools)

HIGHLIGHTS

(All Mehron)   (Cool)

creamy beige   white + yellow   white + red   creamy beige + yellow   creamy beige + purple

Here are all the possible highlights and mixtures of colors to make highlights; this will be a small number and normally these will be *warm*.

SHADOWS

(All Mehron)   (Warm)

terra cotta   contour   purple + terra cotta   blue + terra cotta   terra cotta + maroon

Here are all the possible shadows and mixtures of colors to make shadows; this will be a small number and normally these will be *cool*.

EXPERIMENT!

This area for any experimenting you may want to do to see what variety of colors your kit can make.

SUPPLIERS

The stage makeup products that I use most frequently are made by the four manufacturers listed below. The fifth listing is a retail firm that sells products made by many companies. If you have trouble finding the items you need in your town, contact the following:

Ben Nye, Inc.
5935 Bowcroft Street
Los Angeles, CA 90016
phone (310) 839-1984
FAX (310) 839-2640

Bob Kelly Cosmetics
151 West 46th Street
New York, NY 10036
phone (212) 819-0030
FAX (212) 869-0396

Kryolan Corp.
132 Ninth Street
San Francisco, CA 94103
phone (415) 863-9684
FAX (415) 863-9059

Mehron, Inc.
100 Red Schoolhouse Road
Chestnut Ridge, NY 10977
phone (914) 426-1700
FAX (888) 88-MAKEUP

Alcone Company, Inc.
5-49 49th Avenue
Long Island City, NY 11101
phone (718) 361-8373
FAX (718) 729-8296

RECOMMENDED READING

Baker, Patsy. *Wigs and Makeup for Theatre, Television, and Film.* Woburn, Mass.: Butterworth-Heinemann, 1993.

Baygan, Lee. *Makeup for Theatre, Film, and Television: A Step-by-Step Photographic Guide.* New York: Drama Book Publishers, 1982.

Corey, Irene. *The Face Is a Canvas: A Complete Guide to Theatrical Make-up.* Saddle River, N. J.: Prentice Hall, 1987.

Corson, Richard. *Stage Makeup: Eight Edition.* Saddle River, N. J.: Prentice Hall, 1990.

Delamar, Penny. *Complete Make-up Artist.* Evanston: Northwestern University Press, 1995.

Swinfield, Rosemarie. *Stage Makeup: Step-by-Step.* Cincinnati: Betterway Books, F & W Publications, 1995.

Swinfield, Rosemarie. *Period Makeup for the Stage: Step-by-Step.* Cincinnati: Betterway Books, F & W Publications, 1997.

INDEX